A Trader's Money Management System

How to Ensure Profit and Avoid the Risk of Ruin

BENNETT A. McDOWELL

WILEY

John Wiley & Sons, Inc.

Published by John Wiley & Sons, Inc., Hoboken, New Jersey.
Published simultaneously in Canada.

For general information on our other products and services or for technical support, please contact our Customer Care Department within the United States at (800) 762-2974, outside the United States at (317) 572-3993, or fax (317) 572-4002.

Wiley also publishes its books in a variety of electronic formats. Some content that appears in print may not be available in electronic books. For more information about Wiley products, visit our Web site at www.wiley.com.

Library of Congress Cataloging-in-Publication Data:

McDowell, Bennett, 1957–
    A trader's money management system : how to ensure profit and avoid the risk of ruin / Bennett A. McDowell.
        p.   cm. – (Wiley trading series)
    Includes index.
    ISBN 978-0-470-18771-5 (cloth)
    1. Investment analysis.   2. Speculation.   3. Risk management.   I. Title.
    HG4529.M386   2008
    332.64'5–dc22   2008006155

This book is dedicated with affection to the memory of my father, Robert Adams McDowell, and to my mother, Frances Furqueron McDowell. I am thankful to you both for your guidance, love, and support.

Contents

Foreword

If you use technical analysis, you are likely—or will be likely—to use candle charts. This is because candles can be used in any time frame and in any market, and they allow traders to spot turns before potentially large moves.

As the one who revealed this charting method to the Western world, it is gratifying to see its popularity. However, with the candle charts' universal availability and widespread use, there comes a downside—most traders are using them incorrectly. That is the reason my firm has such a strong focus on education (www.candlecharts.com/free-education).

One of the most dangerous and common misuses of candles is trying to use them as a stand-alone trading vehicle. This is wrong. Candles are a tool, not a trading system. This is why I also show how to combine candles with Western technical tools and to always incorporate risk/reward analysis.

Equally important is money management—that is, proper trade size. For example, what is the proper trade size to enter a position? How do you scale into or out of a trade? How do you adjust trade size for your risk tolerance level? These are important questions, but they are beyond the scope of my expertise. That is why I am pleased to strongly recommend this excellent book.

Based on working with some of the top institutional traders, I can tell you that many of the most successful ones have had more losses than gains. How did they accomplish this? The answer is by the judicious use of stops and proper trade size. So if you are picking up this book, congratulations: You have taken the first steps in following in the footsteps of such successful traders.

There is a Japanese Samurai saying, *"He whose ranks are united in purpose will be victorious."* By merging the timing advantages of candles with the discipline of proven money management as revealed in *A Trader's Money Management System*, you will become a more confident and successful trader. As an extra bonus, you will have less stress!

STEVE NISON
President of Candlecharts.com
Author of *Japanese Candlestick Charting Techniques*
www.candlecharts.com

Preface

M oney management may very well be the most dramatically important piece of the trading success puzzle. The fact that many a sizable fortune (including a couple of small fortunes of my own) have been lost due to the lack of some simple risk control procedures is proof enough for me that this is important stuff.

And yet time and time again, I am reminded that the general population is just not in love with this subject matter. My very own experience reflects this phenomenon, since money management did not take precedence in my career until after my concentration on trade selections and entries were distracted by a couple of huge losses.

So, my conclusion is that it is not usually "love at first sight" with money management—which I'm guessing means that you, the reader, are probably beyond the novice phase. You looked at the title of the book *A Trader's Money Management System* and said, "This is a good book for me." You already know that, yeah, risk control is important. And if you are in the novice category right now, you are well ahead of the game by respecting the value of risk control early on.

What you need to know is that from this book you will get some time-tested techniques that can turn a losing trader into a winning one, and take the winning trader to an entirely new level. Plus, my inclination is to give you as many tools as possible so that you will have the greatest probabilities of success in designing a successful risk control system.

The two important tools you'll get are The Trade Size Calculator software (a one month trial) and The Trader's Assistant record keeping materials (which you can photocopy from the book).

These two tools complement the text and give you a complete package that can deliver results to your bottom line. That's the ultimate goal—greater profits. Enjoy the book. I wish you prosperity and happiness in your trading and all you do!

BENNETT A. MCDOWELL
San Diego, California
March 2008

Acknowledgments

As always, a very special thank you goes to my editor David Pugh at John Wiley & Sons. David, your publishing expertise enhances every project you work on, and I look forward to continuing a long and rewarding relationship. Also, thank you to Kelly O'Connor and Stacey Fischkelta at Wiley: Your guidance and help in every step of the manuscript process is much appreciated.

Thank you to Steve Nison, the greatest candlestick expert of our time, for writing the Foreword. And, much thanks to Professor Nauzer Balsara for allowing us to include one of his risk-of-ruin tables in this book. His classic *Money Management Strategies for Futures Traders*, John Wiley & Sons, 1992, continues to contain the most extensive and thorough set of risk-of-ruin tables in existence.

Many of my students have helped me develop effective educational material over the years by giving their feedback on what helps them most in their learning process. My thanks go out to each and every one. In particular, I'd like to thank Yves Pitteloud, who has been a spectacular student. His insights and contributions in particular to the record keeping portion of this book are terrific.

And, of course, thanks to my wife Jean McDowell, who has been there by my side templating and editing this material every step of the way. Thanks, sweetheart, for all you do—you are much appreciated!

BENNETT A. McDOWELL
San Diego, California
March 2008

Disclaimer

The information in this book, *A Trader's Money Management System*, is intended for educational purposes only. Traders and investors are strongly advised to do their own research and testing to determine the validity of any trading idea or system.

Trading in the financial markets involves substantial risk, and TradersCoach.com, Bennett A. McDowell, or affiliates assume no responsibility for your success or failure in trading or investing in the markets. For this reason, you should only use money you can afford to risk. Furthermore, past performance does not guarantee future results. Thus, even if you were successful with your trading and investing in the past, you may not be successful in the future. TradersCoach.com and Bennett A. McDowell make no performance representation or guarantee of any kind or nature. TradersCoach.com encourages you to conduct your own research and engage in numerous practice trades prior to risking any actual money.

Hypothetical or simulated performance results have certain inherent limitations. Unlike an actual performance record, simulated results do not represent actual trading. Also, since trades have not actually been executed, results may have under- or overcompensated for the impact, if any, of certain market factors, such as lack of liquidity. Simulated trading programs and ideas in general are also subject to the fact that they are designed with the benefit of hindsight. No representation is being made that any account will, or is likely to, achieve profits or losses similar to those discussed.

This Is My Money Management System

This book, *a Trader's Money Management System* is my personal approach to staying out of trouble in the financial markets and maximizing my profits. It's a comprehensive strategy that will take you from the psychology of risk control to the finer aspects of setting stop-loss exits and the value of managing trade size, to record keeping. Finally, it is a step-by-step guide on how to put together a personal system that works for you.

Although many books on money management can be heavily focused on the *mathematical formulas* and *mathematical theories* of risk management, I'm going to try to keep it simple and make the concepts as easy to understand as possible. That way you can see the dramatic benefit of these concepts quickly.

The Resources appendix at the back of this book has a list of terrific (and not so simple) books that I recommend on the mathematical formulas if you decide you want to delve deeper. They are the basis of many of the techniques discussed here.

THE MAIN GOAL IS TO START NOW!

My goal is to get you started sooner rather than later with a system that is workable, so that you can immediately benefit from the value of managing your risk. If you don't have any system in place right now, then this is the perfect time to get it right. And, if there are a few areas in your current system that need attention to get you to the next level, let's work on that.

It's been my observation for many years in working with traders and investors all over the world that risk control tends to be the last piece of the puzzle that most people focus on. Usually, trading entry strategies, software, and systems win first place in the popularity contest—maybe because the belief is that the "system" will generate great fortunes.

Ultimately, a system alone won't create great riches. In addition to the system, traders and investors need to develop discipline and a strong financial psychology, and they must be working with true risk capital—money they can afford to lose. Plus, they need a sound money management system to maximize their system profits and keep them out of financial danger.

EXPECT THE UNEXPECTED

There is a world of risk out there, and managing it is a lifetime endeavor. Every time you get in the car, you risk the possibility of having an automobile accident. When you walk in a thunderstorm, you risk getting hit by lightning (a remote risk, but a risk nonetheless). You may face certain medical risks (which vary, depending on genetic and family history) or risk of losing your job—the list can go on and on.

Typically, in our society, we attempt to control or manage these risks by obtaining insurance, or by using greater care in our day-to-day behavior and choices. For example, you may very well currently have an insurance policy that protects you from auto theft, collision, and bodily injury. You might have medical, life, homeowners, or unemployment insurance. And if you are really responsible, you probably exercise, eat right, and look both ways before you cross the street.

All these precautions and procedures are designed to reduce, not eliminate, the possibility of being devastated by a variety of unexpected circumstances. And that is just the point: These circumstances are unexpected. Our job as traders is to make a habit of expecting and being prepared for the unexpected.

In addition, we need to avoid a state of "trader paralysis" that can be created by unexpected events. If we are well prepared we are better equipped to combat the fear that trading can trigger.

SIX TYPES OF RISK TO MANAGE IN TRADING

In the spirit of expecting the unexpected, we can always attempt to plan for what might happen. In doing so, there are half a dozen primary types of risk for you to consider every time you place a trade. We will cover each of these in detail in the coming chapters, but ponder the following top six for now:

1. Trade risk
2. Market risk
3. Margin risk
4. Liquidity risk
5. Overnight risk
6. Volatility risk

THE LAYOUT OF THIS BOOK

This book is laid out in five parts, all designed to help you develop your own money management system. Following is a summary of the parts so you will have an understanding of where to get what you need at any given point along the way. Make the book work for you. Refer to the table of contents if you want to dive in to one specific topic, you can fluidly move from one part of the material to the other, depending on your experience level and needs.

Part One: Psychology of Risk Control

The mind is a powerful piece of the puzzle in our quest for financial success. There are times when we can be our own worst enemy. Missed opportunities, poor choices, and angry rebellion at the market can all create disaster.

And it is working on the underlying psychology that drives our trading and investing choices that can be the magic key that helps us break through stagnant or nonexistent profits. Here you will see what issues to look for and how to address them in order to more effectively implement your money management system.

Part Two: Stop-Loss Exits

If I had a nickel for every time a trader e-mailed me about losing large sums of money and not having a stop-loss exit in place—well, I'd have a lot of nickels! In any event, sometimes it isn't that an individual doesn't know they need a stop-loss exit in place; instead it's that they don't know how to effectively choose one. Or, they choose one and then don't adhere to it for psychological reasons (see Part One).

In Part Two, we'll clearly take you through a variety of stop-loss approaches and give you tips on how to make sure you do adhere to them when they are hit.

Part Three: Trade Size Does Matter

Are you trading the same exact number of shares on every trade every time, without examining the current market dynamics? It is neat and tidy to have a nice round number of shares or contracts (100 or 1000), but it might not be in your best interest to do so. The concern is that you may be taking on too much risk for certain market conditions.

In this section, you'll learn how to determine how large (or small) your trade size should be so that you are not overextending your risk. You'll even be able to download the *Trade Size Calculator*™ software (a one-month trial is included in your purchase of this book) to see how easy and fast it is to calculate the best trade size for each trade.

Part Four: Record Keeping and Profit/Loss Analysis

Record keeping may not be your favorite pastime, but it is crucial and will pay you significant dividends down the road. If you truly detest the practice of tallying up your profits and losses, that may be a reflection of you hiding from your results.

This brings us back to the psychology of money management. Many emotions can be generated by the simple process of adding up the numbers. This process can commonly generate fear. Fear of success (yes, it is common to be fearful when you are actually successful at something like trading), and fear of failure can be all too familiar.

Now is when you need to gather every molecule of discipline you have and start running the numbers. This doesn't mean waiting until the end of the month and getting your calculator out. It means every day, tally up the numbers. It's the only way to stay honest and accountable.

To get started on your recordkeeping, we've include diagrams in the book of all the trade posting cards and trade ledgers that are in *The Trader's Assistant*, which has been honored with *Stocks & Commodities* magazine's Readers Choice Award. You can photocopy these forms right from the book and get started.

Part Five: Design Your Own Plan

This is the fun part. Here you get to customize your own plan to fit your risk tolerance, your experience level, and your financial needs. We'll walk you through the money management techniques at your disposal and will help you to design a realistic plan. This plan is one that you will continue to use and profit from.

GET YOUR HIGHLIGHTER OUT AND USE IT

Are you ready to get started? Don't be afraid to write in this book (unless you are borrowing it from the library or a friend!). Jot down ideas along the way of how to apply these techniques to your trading system.

The beauty of a sound money management system like the one in this book is that it can be used in conjunction with *any* trading or investing system. These concepts are universal and will serve you well. If you have any questions on the material you are about to read, please contact me at Team@TradersCoach.com.

Good trading to you today, tomorrow, and always!

BENNETT A. MCDOWELL
San Diego, California
March 2008

Psychology of Risk Control

CHAPTER 1

It Just Ain't Sexy!

M oney management probably doesn't come up as the number-one item on your top-ten list of fun things to study. That is, not until you start making money as a result of getting really good at it. The key for every trader is to discover the financial benefit to sound money management—and then all of a sudden, it becomes totally fun. Once you see how effective sound money management can be at ensuring profit and avoiding the risk of ruin, it might just become your favorite part of trading!

WHY IS MONEY MANAGEMENT SO BORING?

Upon hearing the term *money management*, you may think, "Why does money management have to be so boring?" Well, maybe that's because it's so much more exciting to get into a financial market with a flurry of activity and not a care in the world. And it's just that kind of behavior that gets the average novice trader into trouble because they don't yet own the perception that risk analysis and money management really is important.

Isn't it much more fun to dream of the phenomenal huge financial outcome of one's newly entered trade than to plan for the seemingly remote possibility that there could be financial loss? After all, why be negative?

At first glance, it seems that placing a trade and getting in the game is thrill enough in itself. What more could you ask for? That is, what more could you ask for, until the position unexpectedly goes in the wrong direction, generating a loss of capital. But, that's only a paper loss you say, since the market will surely get back on track and go in the right direction. No problem!

Then it seems the market is not being cooperative, and for some reason, it does not comply with the plan (of making lots of quick cash) and it does *not* go in the desired direction. Instead, it continues in exactly the *wrong* direction. Isn't that when the thrill of entering a great position instead becomes the anxiety of wondering how to get out of a not-so-great position? Of course, the adrenaline kicks in, the heart rate increases, sweaty palms appear, and the physical metamorphosis from thrill to dread quickly evolves.

So, let's see, the position instantly gaps—again, it's going in the wrong direction. How can this be? That gut feeling was so clear and compelling when we entered the trade. It was a sure thing, wasn't it? We couldn't have been wrong, could we? Now at this point, the trade is so far gone, we can't afford to get out, can we?

Most of this evolution of a position gone bad has to do with entering the market and risking real cash without having a plan, a stop, and a tested money management system—*before* the entry.

It's a pretty common occurrence, actually. It's happened to the best of us. There are many reasons that it happens—ignorance, impatience, inability to admit we might be wrong, inexperience, or, worst of all reasons, an addiction to the adrenaline rush of taking on a position (for better or worse).

Regardless of the reason, I'm guessing that most of us would agree, it's not all that sexy to lose money. It's not much fun, either. The question is, do we find it painful enough to change our thinking and implement a money management plan now, or will it take another loss or two to bring the concept home?

The answer to that question is different for everyone.

PSYCHOLOGY OF RISK CONTROL

The psychology of risk control sooner or later begins with genuinely believing that you will benefit from a risk control plan. Then, it's a matter of directing your resources toward that goal. Regarding resources, you'll need to devote time to design a plan, allocate some money for purchasing tools and materials that will assist you, and then, most importantly, focus your emotional energy on rethinking how you look at money and the markets.

Maybe you'll be one of the few lucky ones who will own the belief that risk control is important right off the bat. More often than not though, most traders learn this lesson the hard way—by losing money. Regardless, developing your risk control psychology will be a crucial key in developing a personal money management plan that works.

When you've mastered your psychology, you'll experience less anxiety and will be able to implement your plan more consistently. There are often times when traders will design a terrific plan that emotionally they don't adhere to because their psychology is not fully developed. It takes time, but as the profits increase, resulting from a sound money management plan, your psychology will gradually strengthen.

STEP NUMBER ONE: MAKE IT SEXY AND MAKE IT FUN

To begin with, making money is sexy and making money is fun. So, if you can translate these two understandings into a money management system, you'll be way ahead of the game. For example, instead of dreading a *stop out* (which, by the way, is a natural part of trading) when your system tells you the trade has gone bad, think of it as getting one step closer to the winning trade.

From a probability standpoint, if your system generates six winners for every four losers, then the sooner you get the losers out of the way, the sooner you'll get to ride one of the winners. That's a whole lot more fun than focusing on some insignificant monetary loss from a stop out.

When I say insignificant, that's because what we'll be covering in the following pages is a strategy where all of your stop-loss exits will be set at a point where the most you will lose on any one trade will be 2 percent of your trading account. That is a manageable loss, and on a $10,000 trading account the most you will lose on any single trade will be $200. Not too bad, right?

By limiting your loss potential on each and every trade, you will reduce the anxiety associated with stop-outs and will automatically strengthen your psychology.

IMPORTANT NOTE: For some advanced traders, it is beneficial to risk more than 2 percent of their trading account. The amount these traders risk must be carefully calculated depending on their proven historical performance statistics. See Chapter 9 for the formulas to determine if your payoff ratio and win ratio performance warrant a higher risk than 2 percent.

FEAR AND GREED ARE NOT THE ONLY EMOTIONS IN TRADING

In the movie *Wall Street*, Gordon Gecko says, "Greed. . .is good." Gordon may be a bit overzealous in his love of greed, but that is certainly an entertaining scene in the movie!

When the psychology of the markets is discussed, fear and greed are often the most common emotions that are bantered about. And yet, there are a number of other, equally important emotions in play.

Here are some *negative* psychological motivators (other than fear and greed) to consider when evaluating your own trading psychology:

- Regret
- Anxiety
- Blame
- Dread
- Anger
- Apathy
- Denial

Here are some *positive* psychological motivators to consider when evaluating your own trading psychology:

- Happiness
- Acceptance
- Anticipation
- Pride
- Appreciation
- Confidence

When evaluating your psychological and emotional motivators, you want to focus on ways in which you can reduce the occurrence of negative emotions and increase the occurrence of positive emotions. You may not decrease all the negatives, and you may not increase all the positives, but the growth goal is to strive in this direction.

PSYCHOLOGICAL MOTIVATORS

We're all driven by both positive and negative psychological motivators. What a sound money management system will do for you is diminish your negative motivators and increase your positive motivators.

For example, if you know that the most you'll lose on your $10,000 account is $200 on any one trade, that decreases and relieves an enormous amount of anxiety. Stress and anxiety are negative motivators, and the less of these you have, the more profitable you will be (and the more you will enjoy your trading).

As you gain confidence in your plan, you will begin to see your profits increase. There is a certain amount of pride that comes from generating greater profits on each trade, and that increased pride is a positive psychological motivator.

These are just a couple of illustrations of how to view your psychology. Ideally, you want to look at your own personality and emotional tendencies to determine which negative and positive emotions you experience while trading. The goal is to enjoy the process of trading—to decrease any negative emotions you may have and increase the positive ones.

CHAPTER 2

Confidence in Your Plan

I f you don't believe your plan will work, it won't. That's a rule that applies to most anything, kind of a self-fulfilling prophecy. Many things may stand in your way, a good plan but poor self esteem, an ego that doesn't think you need a plan, or maybe just a poor plan. If you don't believe in your plan (or don't have one), get to the bottom why and make adjustments; it is now or never.

YOU GOTTA' BELIEVE!

One of the greatest challenges for any trader is to finally come to the point where he or she sincerely believes to the very core of their being that a sound money management program is vital.

It is a stumbling block for a great many, since most individuals participating in the markets today just don't believe that money management is particularly important. Analyzing the crucial and latest fundamentals, using the best technical software, most traders and investors believe that those items are the magic pill and should take priority over and above everything else. They think money management "just ain't sexy."

It's one of those things where a trader is convinced, "What happened to that guy, that'll never happen to me. I'm smarter than that, I would never lose that much money. I'm not that stupid—my fundamental and technical analysis is flawless..."

Truthfully, to satisfy your ego's need for feeling brilliant, it's all a matter of probabilities and has nothing to do with being "smart" or "stupid."

Frankly, it could happen to anyone, because the market is a volatile, powerful and unpredictable place. The power of the market can overcome even the most experienced of market participants. Sometimes, it's like a tidal wave—you may even see it coming but you can't get out of the way in time.

The 1929 and 1987 market crashes, the many housing bubbles over the years, Pearl Harbor, September 11, the technology bubble of 2000, the collapse of Enron—the list goes on and on. Some situations are bigger than life, and it is those situations, in addition to the day-to-day unpredictable nature of the market, that sound risk control can help you manage. It is all about calculating probabilities and making sure they work for you and not against you.

It is similar to having an insurance policy—so, yes, your house burned down or got blown away in a hurricane. But at least you have insurance money to rebuild your life once you have overcome the emotional shock and devastation. A stop-loss exit will cost you money along the way just like the cost of insurance, but you didn't lose it all and you can regroup and rethink your position at the end of the day.

Consider that position in contrast to not having a stop loss in place and instantly losing everything you have. Basically, a money management plan is a cost of doing business, just like insurance that you no doubt currently have and understand the need for. Consider a change in perspective and see money management as insurance and a cost of doing business. It may take on an even greater meaning and value to you.

AN INSURANCE POLICY FOR TRADERS AND INVESTORS

The principles that work for you in day-to-day life can also work in your trading and investing endeavors. Putting a money management plan into place may create some additional costs to you in both time and money. But these costs can work to your advantage in the same way as paying a monthly insurance premium cost can protect you against catastrophe for a variety of situations in your day-to-day life.

We've listed a number of common insurance policies that you may be benefiting from today. If you can see how these policies help protect you from disaster, you may find it easier to see the benefit in also insuring that you protect yourself from the potential risks that are inherent in the financial markets:

- Automobile insurance for both bodily injury and car repair and replacement due to an accident

- Home insurance for both bodily injury and home repair and replacement due to an accident or catastrophe

- Health insurance for everyday illnesses and routine check-ups, as well as catastrophic and terminal illness
- Life insurance protection for the devastating loss of a loved one that may be a provider, so that the family can deal with their grief and have their monetary needs provided for
- Disability insurance if one becomes unable to work due to physical or medical complications and can't generate income to provide for necessities

In the final analysis, by implementing an insurance plan, you are protecting yourself from the worst-case scenario. You are limiting your risk and ensuring that you will not be completely devastated in the event of a catastrophic event that you have little or no control over. Basically, it means you can come back to play the game another day instead of being completely wiped out.

Yes, if you are affected by any of these devastating accidents, illnesses, or account drawdown, there are certainly emotional and financial issues to recover from, but they are set at a stop-loss limit that controls your risk of ruin.

THE "AMAT" TRADE THAT GOT AWAY

Many years ago when I was trading Applied Materials, stock symbol AMAT, I placed a trade that went out of control and completely got away from me. Ironically, the financial loss incurred was the most expensive lesson I'd learned by far, and yet it provided me with my most valuable lesson in risk control and in controlling my anger at the markets.

Applied Materials was range bound for quite some time on the daily chart. News on the stock was negative, and my forecasting analysis indicated a shorting opportunity, so I shorted Applied Materials by selling call options. Over the next week, Applied Materials began one of its biggest upward moves it had seen in the prior three months.

I didn't exit the trade. Instead, I rationalized (or should I say, fantasized) that this upward move was just a quick move to the upside before selling off. After all, my forecasting analysis was still indicating lower prices, and there was no new news event that could account for this upward bullish move.

So, I just hung in there while attempting to calm myself down and hoping it was still okay. The next week, I watched in disbelief as Applied Materials kept moving sharply upward. There had not been a move this strong in years on this stock. That is when the shock, fear, and anxiety set in.

I was currently down about $25,000, and did not know what to do. I wanted to get out, but didn't want to take a loss that large. It seemed the only choice I had was to hang in there and stay with the position. The emotions created by this trade gone bad clouded and paralyzed my judgment.

On week three, the upward surge continued, and by that Friday I had experienced my limit of anxiety. Not being able to take one more second of pain as I watched my loss grow to an absurd level, I exited the trade. I lost $30,000 in just three weeks on one trade.

I was so angry I wanted to get even with the market, especially this particular stock. So, I immediately went long to recoup my money by buying into the uptrend. The next day, the trend reversed, and I watched for the next week as my long positions lost money. I finally got out of my long position with a loss of $2,000. I was devastated financially and emotionally. Trading was not fun anymore. I had lost a total of $32,000 in just four weeks.

I took some time off, and recouped. Once I regained my senses, I analyzed the trade. It took me awhile before I could look at this trade objectively without getting angry. In the final analysis, if I had used stops and adhered to them, I would have keep my loss small. I also would have been able to clearly see the new uptrend developing and would have been able to enter it early on.

Also, using stops would have kept me objective and in control of myself and my trading. From that point on, I learned that risk control through stop-loss setting and proper *trade size* was essential. It took a large hit like this AMAT loss, along with a devastating blow to my psyche, before I learned this lesson about risk control on a deep level. Some people say that no one can fully appreciate the need for risk control until they personally experience a serious financial loss. It is my hope that maybe, by hearing first-hand stories like mine, you will recognize the need without first-hand experiencing the financial loss yourself—that is, if you haven't already learned the expensive way. The markets are the ultimate university of finance and sometimes the tuition is on par with Harvard, Columbia, or Yale.

A PENNY STOCK TRADE THAT WENT BANKRUPT

This trade was an interesting trade for me, and again it was many years back. My entry was based on buying a penny stock that the analysts and my investment newsletters all said was the best penny stock to buy. The stock was at approximately 75 cents, so I bought about 30,000 shares, which amounted to $22,500.

My rationale was this: The newsletter that was recommending this stock had done extensive analysis. The few analysts I could find following this stock did not have anything bad to say. The stock was at its 52-week low, so how much lower could it go? I was not going to be greedy, because as soon as the stock got to a dollar, I would start selling it and take my profit. I did not see any sense in using stops because the stock was so cheap anyway. So I just decided to let it ride until it got to one dollar, then I would sell.

The first week the penny stock price rose, and I was ecstatic. I already had a profit—that newsletter really knew how to pick them. Then, about a week later, it started to move slowly back down to the price I bought it at. Oh well, I thought, back to where I started, no big deal. That must have been the first upward price surge; next surge would be to a dollar, no problem.

The stock bounced between about 62 cents and 80 cents for approximately two more weeks, and then boom—it fell to 30 cents with news that the CEO was quitting and funding was drying up for this company. Liquidity was low, and even if I wanted to sell, I was not sure I could sell my 30,000 shares. I decided to do nothing, since maybe this stock would bounce back. Well, to make a long story short, it eventually went bankrupt, and I lost my entire $22,500.

The lesson learned here is that there is risk and opportunity in every trade or investment we make. Be sure to trade markets that have enough liquidity so you can control your risk. And, of course, always have a stop-loss exit in place because, yes, the price can go lower—it can even go to zero.

THAT'S WHEN I BECAME A BELIEVER AND DEVELOPED CONFIDENCE IN MY PLAN

The point in me telling you those two early experiences in having trades go bad is that the monetary (and emotional) pain and suffering of these specific trades with AMAT and the penny stock is what gave me the motivation to develop a thorough money management system that has kept me on the right track ever since.

Those two losses are what enabled me to own the heartfelt belief that risk management was essential to consistent financial success. You may have the best system and approach in the world and it may earn you great revenue, but if you give it all back on a few bad trades, then you've defeated the entire purpose.

So, yes, I am now a money management believer, heart and soul. And it is that belief that gives me confidence in the plan that I've developed. Over the years, my plan has proven to me that it is far better to take a few small losses than to take the big hits that are inevitable when you've got no plan or an ineffective plan.

THE CALIFORNIA WILDFIRES ARE RAGING TONIGHT

As I write this, the October Santa Ana winds are blowing the palm trees outside to a tune of 70 miles an hour (that is nearly hurricane level). We're based here in San Diego, California, and as I speak there are 17 separate fires raging across the state, the worst in history.

Mother Nature is a powerful and unpredictable force (much like the financial markets that we trade in) and she is relentless tonight. We haven't been evacuated yet, but since we live on a hilltop up on a canyon, we have a front row seat to watch the "Witch Fire," as it is called, advance in our direction. At present it is about 5 miles away, a raging orange glow along the hills in the black darkness.

There is no way to know if the fires will ultimately reach us (again unpredictable, just like the markets), but the cars are packed with essentials like bedding, food, water, clothing, and some toys for the kids. The wind could change direction, it could intensify, or it could calm down. There is just no way to tell for sure, and like the markets, the best plan is to accept where it is right this minute and not try to predict the future.

With that said, we are certainly prepared for the worst-case scenario and have already mentally played out the "war games" so that we can minimize the downside if we should lose the house. That means having a plan that includes homeowners' insurance to rebuild if necessary, having the cars packed in advance so we can get the family out of danger, and watching the direction that the fires are moving every step of the way.

My wife, Jean, and I will take shifts tonight to watch the hill, and if it gets to a certain point we've agreed on, that's when we'll evacuate. Sure sounds like an "exit" stop loss, doesn't it? As long as our family members are safe, the loss of material items is secondary. We have some experience with this fire plan, since we survived the "Cedar Fire" here only four years ago. Sadly, the Cedar Fire devastated our area. In our zip code of 92131, San Diego, there were 1,200 single-family homes standing before the fire. When the final count was taken, and after the fire was put out by countless brave firefighters, one third of those homes were completely burned to the ground. That comes to 400 homes in a seven-mile radius—gone.

We were among the lucky ones, and our street was completely untouched. But, many of our friends were affected by this heartbreaking event. In the region (outside our zip code area), another 1,000 homes were also lost. Yes, 90 percent of those who lost their homes did rebuild.

An odd thing to note about the nature of the fires is that they seem to have a mind of their own. They even create their own weather system and wind direction. When you would look at an area the Cedar Fire had moved through after the fire was over, it seemed almost random, as the fire would destroy a row of houses and then in the middle of the row, there would be one lone house standing completely untouched.

Who could predict or explain why that one house escaped the devastation? No one can explain, not even the firefighters. They will tell you that the fire moves where it wants to, and sometimes seems to have no logic other than its own powerful path. Again, it is much like the markets, since there are times that they, too, seem to defy logic.

How timely for these fires to occur just as I am working on this book. The similarities between Mother Nature and the markets are dramatic. They are both powerful and unpredictable, but they are manageable. The value of bringing up this wildfire experience is to illustrate how there are risks all around us that we are managing every day. Some risks are more catastrophic than others, but the idea is to use the same common sense that you would use in managing your day-to-day risks—use that common sense in your trading.

Editor's Note: The author's house survived the "Witch Fire of 2007," but this fire was so devastating that the area was declared to be in a federal state of emergency: 500,000 people were evacuated with the reverse 911 telephone announcement system (the largest evacuation in history); 1,700 homes and structures were destroyed.

Risk—that's what this book and trading is all about. It's about taking on calculated risks that you can profit from. And the only way to profit consistently is to have a plan to manage your risk and assess your risk—effectively. So now the question to you is, do you truly believe that you need a money management system? When your answer to this question is yes, you will be able to design a sound money management system that will ensure profit and avoid the risk of ruin.

CHAPTER 3

Yin and Yang

Our world is made up of opposites, yin and yang, dark and light, weakness and strength. These opposites drive your trading psychology every day. Understanding these opposites will enable you to gain insight into the forces of your unconscious that are at work as you place trades in the markets. Being that these forces are unconscious, it takes a little introspection to see them and understand them. In the following pages, you'll be looking in the mirror to identify these unconscious forces to see how they may impact your trading psychology. The more that you know and understand yourself, the better a trader you will be.

FOCUS ON YOUR STRENGTHS AND ADJUST FOR YOUR WEAKNESSES

We've all got strengths and weaknesses, even the occasional egomaniac who believes he has only strengths. Providing that you don't fall into the egomaniac category, we'd like you to look at both sides of the equation, so that you can implement a plan that highlights your strengths and prevents your weaknesses from hindering your success.

There are a few ways to look at weaknesses. One way is to realize that sometimes a "perceived" weakness can be turned into a strength. For example, if you have a high level of fear, you may channel that fear into action by focusing your energies on exceptional preparation for the trade and for entering the market. Once you can cultivate your confidence level (with

23

repeated small successes), that skill in preparation (which was motivated by a fearful mindset) may be your greatest asset.

Another way to look at a weakness is to realize that our minds are an amazing thing. You can rewire certain thought processes to change your belief system and even change some of your weaknesses. Now, this may not be possible in all cases, but by using certain techniques, it is possible to rewire your brain.

For example, suppose one of your nagging weaknesses is anxiety that creates paralysis and prevents you from implementing your plan. You can rewire your thinking to reduce the anxiety, possibly using relaxation techniques, or you could adjust your trading plan so it is not as aggressive. With behavior modification, the anxiety may simply disappear and may no longer be an issue.

Of course, your strengths are a different matter. You probably know what they are. Maybe your skills with computers are exceptional and make it easy for you to produce fantastic technical charts. Use that asset to your advantage, and work your computer savvy into your plan. Maybe your analysis abilities on fundamentals have an intuitive knack for being on target—so again, work that positive strength into your plan.

Capitalizing on your strengths and weaknesses will develop your risk psychology and will make it easier for you to implement your money management plan more effectively and consistently.

YIN AND YANG OPPOSITES DEFINED

There is a Chinese philosophy of yin and yang that basically illustrates the opposites in our universe, such as strength and weakness. These opposites are very telling. This philosophy believes that there is no such thing as 100 percent black or 100 percent white, and that black and white (and all opposites) coexist in nature in an intertwined harmonious circle shape.

The yin and yang image in Figure 3.1 presents a small white circle floating in the black area and a small black circle floating in the white area. The belief is that there is a little bit of the opposite that exists in every universal element. Characters in a book or movie are never all bad or all good (except maybe on soap operas). There is usually a little diversity thrown into the characters to make them more interesting. The Chinese believe that in the universe, the same applies: Nothing is 100 percent black or white.

With that said, neither yin nor yang is either good or bad; they just are what they are. This is similar to your strengths and weaknesses; they are not necessarily good or bad. Acceptance of what they are is valuable in your progress as a trader in the markets.

FIGURE 3.1 Chinese Yin and Yang Symbol Illustrating Opposites in Harmony

This means that there must be harmony and balance in your approach in order to be consistently successful. For example, excessive joy over a win or excessive anger over a loss will not be beneficial to your financial outcome. Rather, an even keel—a balanced emotional attitude where all your opposites are in harmony—will create the best financial bottom line.

For example, when I had two trades that created huge monetary losses for me many years ago, it seemed like that was the worst thing that could happen. I was angry at myself for sure. But, just as in the Chinese philosophy, that dark moment created the seed for a bright future that included the sound money management that I use to this day. Now that I have distance from those losses, I can see objectively that they were the catalyst that created a plan that generates far more monetary gains in the here and now. My perception of the early losses has changed.

Take a look at Table 3.1. What I want you to see is that there are many opposites in this world that live in harmony. Dark, light; weakness, strength; downward, upward; bear market, bull market; these opposites all coexist and operate together. It is as if without one of them, the other would not exist.

My point in providing this list of yin and yang is for you to see that you need not fear your weaknesses. And, just as important, you need not

TABLE 3.1   Table of Yin and Yang Opposites

YIN	YANG
Weakness	Strength
Downward	Upward
Bear Market	Bull Market
Passive	Active
Moon	Sun
Black	White
Dark	Light
Soft	Hard
Cold	Hot
Quiet	Loud
Submissive	Dominant
Even	Odd
Inward	Outward
Water	Fire
Earth	Heaven
Feminine	Masculine

glorify your strengths. Instead, embrace them both and use them both to enhance your trading performance. Just the introspective understanding of your personal attributes will put you in a powerful position. This introspection will enable you to develop a strong yin and yang psychology where you create a harmonious relationship between all of your perceived strengths and weaknesses.

Trading and success in the financial markets is not merely about having an exceptional approach or system that will give you an *edge*. Rather, it is about having an exceptional understanding of yourself, along with the system that will give you your edge. This exceptional understanding will lead to attaining *the trader's mindset.*

YIN AND YANG PERCEPTIONS REVEALED

When you look at the list of yin and yang opposites in Table 3.1, you may say to yourself at first glance, "the left column has all *bad* weaknesses and right column has all *good* strengths." Herein lies the impact of your perceptions. In reality there are no entirely good or bad traits, sometimes a perceived weakness can turn into a unique asset. It is all in how you perceive and approach the world.

The Chinese philosophy preaches not good or bad per se, but instead harmony amongst opposites. For example, characteristics sometimes perceived as bad such as weakness, and a submissive and passive nature ironically can be an asset in the world of a trader. In the industry, it is frequently discussed that women are better traders than men. It is their natural ability to be passive and flow with the market as opposed to being strong and fighting the market that enables them to generate greater profits.

Another interesting observation is that yin can be stronger than yang. When you look at the yin characteristic of water it is in fact considered stronger than the yang characteristic of fire. This is because water can extinguish fire and for this reason has greater power. The value of discussing these philosophies is so that you can look at yourself with greater understanding and awareness.

And remember that nothing is entirely black and white. Choose your perceptions carefully and consider that sometimes perceived weaknesses, if approached creatively, can be transformed into strengths. It is all in how you approach these inner qualities and characteristics that will determine the outcome.

IDENTIFY YOUR CURRENT STRENGTHS AND WEAKNESSES

So now we want to take a look in the mirror and determine what we currently see. Don't identify what was there ten years ago (a few less wrinkles, perhaps), or what you hope to see tomorrow, but what you see right now. This exercise of taking inventory will help us later when we are ready to develop our plan. Check off all the boxes that apply to both your strengths and weaknesses.

Current Strengths
☐ Strong computer skills
☐ Have a current risk plan in place
☐ Tested trading system in use
☐ Ability to identify changing market cycles
☐ Strong analytic skills
☐ Ability to be disciplined
☐ Mathematic and accounting skills
☐ Attention to detail
☐ Problem-solving skills
☐ Ability to pull the trigger

☐ Ability to stay out of the market
☐ Lack of anxiety
☐ Calm under pressure
☐ No anger
☐ Even-keeled emotions
☐ Healthy self-esteem
☐ Desire to improve skills
☐ Enjoyment of the process
☐ Ability to be flexible
☐ Generally optimistic
☐ Realistic risk–reward objectives

Current Weaknesses
☐ Lack of computer skills
☐ No current risk plan in place
☐ No tested trading system in place
☐ Inability to identify changing market cycles
☐ Lack of discipline
☐ Excessive anger
☐ Excessive joy
☐ Excessive anxiety
☐ Excessive greed
☐ Excessive fear
☐ Inability to pull the trigger
☐ Compulsive tendencies
☐ Low self-esteem
☐ Paralysis under pressure
☐ Overtrading
☐ Performance denial
☐ Apathy
☐ Lack of flexibility
☐ Generally pessimistic
☐ Risk adverse
☐ Risk (and thrill) addicted
☐ Unrealistic risk–reward objectives

AFTER YOU TAKE INVENTORY

Once you've taken inventory of your current standing, then you want to decide how to eliminate some of the items on the weakness list and add some new items to the strengths list.

Some of these might be very simple, and you are probably addressing them as we speak. Meaning that you may not currently have a money management plan in place, but that is why you are reading this book, isn't it? So once you have your risk plan completed, you'll already have moved one item from your weak column to your strong column.

Remember, when it comes to weaknesses and strengths, it is all relative. For example, a little fear and greed is actually a good thing. A little fear will give you respect for the power of the market, as long as the fear doesn't overwhelm and paralyze you. A little greed is not so bad, either, since that will motivate you to be creative in developing more profitable approaches. Just keep it all in moderation and maintain a healthy balance where you feel comfortable and not out of control.

Take inventory once a year or so to follow your progress. There will be some traits you won't be able to change, and that is okay. The objective is to increase the number of strengths and decrease the number of weaknesses to the best of your abilities. In some cases, you may be able to turn your weaknesses into strengths.

CHAPTER 4

Risk Psychology and "The Trader's Mindset"

E very great trader has a deep understanding of their own psychology. This personal trading psychology affects every trade entry and every trade exit they make and there is awareness that this psychology is a "work in progress," meaning that even great traders struggle with their inner demons from time to time. Those demons might be fear, greed, or regret. Regardless of what the demons are, the more you develop what we call "The Trader's Mindset" the quicker you will confront your demons and the more success you will have in slaying them.

In every trader's journey from novice trader to master trader and beyond, they need to keep an eye on the ball, and on their trading psychology. Life will present a variety of challenges and each day will be a unique opportunity for you to enhance and further develop The Trader's Mindset. Maybe a severe draw down will test your will or the market will throw you a curve ball. The strength (or lack there of) of your trading psychology will be the one attribute that will set you apart from the trader on the opposite side of your trade.

WE CALL IT "THE TRADER'S MINDSET"

There are certain traits that help traders and investors consistently profit in the markets. Some of these traits will come naturally to each individual, but others will need to be cultivated and acquired. It may take some time before you will attain all these traits, but it begins with knowing what the qualities are that you are looking for.

HERE IS WHAT YOU'LL FEEL AFTER ACQUIRING THE TRADER'S MINDSET

1. Not caring about the money

2. Acceptance of the risk in trading and investing

3. Winning and losing trades accepted equally from an emotional standpoint

4. Enjoyment of the process

5. No feeling of being victimized by the markets

6. Always looking to improve skills

7. Trading and investing account profits now accumulating and flowing in as skills improve

8. Open minded; keeping opinions to a minimum

9. No anger

10. Learning from every trade or position

11. Using one chosen approach or system and not being influenced by the market or other traders

12. No need to conquer or control the market

13. Feeling confident and feeling in control

14. A sense of not forcing the markets

15. Trading with money you can afford to risk

16. Taking full responsibility for all trading results

17. Sense of calmness when trading

18. Ability to focus on the present reality

19. Not caring which way the market breaks or moves

20. Aligning trades in the direction of the market, flowing with the market

FIFTEEN DESTRUCTIVE PSYCHOLOGICAL TRADING ISSUES AND THEIR CAUSES

This list of 15 obstacles to attaining The Trader's Mindset is useful as a reference in troubleshooting. Review this list when you are experiencing drawdown to see if any old bad habits have reappeared or maybe a new obstacle has developed that you have never experienced before. Then see "if the shoe fits" and use the list to determine what approaches you might be able to take to pull yourself out of a performance slump.

This list is not all inclusive; you may experience combinations of the following issues or may have obstacles that are not even on the list. If that is the case, jot down your notes in the "Personal Obstacles" section so that you can create your own diagnosis and solution.

1. *Fear of being stopped out or fear of taking a loss.* The usual reason for this is that the trader fears failure and feels like he or she cannot take another loss. The trader's ego is at stake.

2. *Getting out of trades too early.* Anxiety is relieved by closing a position. This is caused by a fear of position reversing and then feeling let down. The trader has a need for instant gratification.

3. *Wishing and hoping.* The trader does not want to take control or take responsibility for the trade. The trader has an inability to accept the present reality of the marketplace.

4. *Anger after a losing trade.* There is a feeling of being a victim of the markets. Unrealistic expectations lead to caring too much about a specific trade. Tying your self-worth to your success in the markets, or needing approval from the markets, will lead to losses.

5. *Trading with money you cannot afford to lose or trading with borrowed money.* It is desperation to view a trade as the last hope at success. Traders fall into this trap when they are trying to be successful at something or fear losing the chance at opportunity. Other causes are lack of discipline and greed.

6. *Adding on to a losing position (doubling down).* The trader does not want to admit the trade is wrong and hopes it will come back. The trader's ego is at stake.

7. *Compulsive trading.* A trader can be drawn to the excitement of the markets. Addiction and gambling issues are present. Such traders need to feel in the game. They have difficulty when not trading, such as on weekends—they are obsessed with trading.

8. *Excessive joy after a winning trade.* Tying your self-worth to the markets. The trader feels unrealistically "in control" of the markets.

9. *Stagnant or poor trading account profits—limiting profits.* In this situation, a trader might feel undeserving of being successful—of making money or profits. Usually, this involves psychological issues such as poor self-esteem.

10. *Not following your trading system.* The trader doesn't believe it really works, or did not test it well. Maybe it does not match your personality. Maybe you want more excitement in your trading. Or maybe you don't trust your own ability to choose a successful system.

11. *Overthinking the trade—second guessing the trading.* Fear of loss or being wrong can paralyze a trader. A perfectionist personality can create this problem. Causes include wanting a sure thing where sure things don't exist; not understanding that loss is a part of trading and the outcome of each trade is unknown; not accepting there is risk in trading; and not accepting the unknown.

12. *Not trading the correct trade size.* Dreaming the trade will be only profitable. The trader might not fully recognize the risk and not understand the importance of money management. The trader might be refusing to take responsibility for managing the risk, or be too lazy to calculate proper trade size.

13. *Trading too much.* The trader feels a need to conquer the market. Causes include greed and trying to get even with the market for a previous loss. The excitement of trading is similar to compulsive trading, issue number 7.

14. *Afraid to trade.* No trading system in place. The trader is not comfortable with risk and the unknown. The trader might fear total loss or ridicule. The trader might have a need for control. There is no confidence in your trading system or in yourself.

15. *Irritable after the trading day.* The trader is on an emotional roller coaster due to anger, fear, or greed. There is too much attention on trading results and not enough on the process and learning the skill of trading. The trader focuses on the money too much. There are unrealistic trading expectations.

When one of the items in this list occurs, isolate and defuse it ASAP. From time to time issues will arise that you've never encountered, usually during a growth phase when you may be testing a new approach. Identify the issue, acknowledge and adjust. Self awareness is the key and will enable you to maintain profitability.

MIRROR, MIRROR ON THE WALL

Take a look in the mirror and see if you are experiencing any of the 15 destructive psychological trading issues we've listed. This exercise is similar to identifying your strengths and weaknesses (in Chapter 3). It is designed to give you a greater understanding of where you are now, and how to address some of the current negative issues.

Some of these issues will be directly related to designing your money management system. For example, if you are having difficulty with number 12, not trading the correct trade size, you will be able to work on that when we get to Chapter 10.

Make a note of the destructive issues you may be experiencing now, and revisit this section after you have completed your money management plan to see if some of these issues may have corrected themselves.

Ultimately, this list of 15 issues will all be obstacles to obtaining the trader's mindset, so you need to eventually address all of the issues you are struggling with. As you overcome each issue, you will be one step closer to attaining *nirvana*—or The Trader's Mindset.

PERSONAL OBSTACLES

Use this area to jot down what you learned about the obstacles that may be holding you back. If any of the items in the list of 15 are creating trouble for you now, then list them in the lines below and specify what you can do to address the obstacle. If there are issues that do not appear in the list of 15, then write in what they are below so that you can mentally and emotionally confront these issues now.

☐ Obstacle and Solution:

_____

_____

_____

_____

_____

_____

_____

☐ Obstacle and Solution:

_____

_____

_____

_____

_____

_____

_____

☐ Obstacle and Solution:

_____

_____

_____

_____

_____

_____

_____

_____

☐ Obstacle and Solution:

_____

_____

_____

_____

_____

_____

_____

NIRVANA IS WHERE YOU WANT TO BE

Nirvana is a place or condition of great peace and bliss, make that your goal
and it will become your reality. In essence, attaining The Trader's Mindset
is getting to a place of profitability, peace and bliss. Just the action of writing what your obstacles are right now will bring you one step closer to
acquiring nirvana.

PART TWO

Stop-Loss Exits

CHAPTER 5

Not Every Trade Will be a Winner

There is no such thing as 100 percent perfection on this planet—not as long as the human factor is in play. Given this fact, and recognizing that this fact applies to trading, we need to plan for the inevitable. And the inevitable involves loss, account drawdown, and the peaks and valleys of trading. Can you weather the valleys long enough to enjoy the peaks? That will depend on how well you manage your risk and manage the fact that not every trade will be a winner.

Gambling casinos understand that not every game of poker or blackjack will go in their favor and be a winner for the house. In fact, they have no idea which hand played will be a winner or loser. But, they do know that they have a winning edge over the public playing at their casino and over time they know they will win more than they lose. It is a game of probabilities, just as in trading.

OVERSTATING THE OBVIOUS?

After reading this chapter title, you may be asking yourself, "Isn't he stating the obvious?" That may be true, but it is important to visit this seemingly obvious statement. Depending on your personal experience level, novice to intermediate to master, you will have a varying understanding of this statement.

The masters will have a deeper understanding of loss and losing trades. They no doubt already know their ratio of wins to losses, average dollar win to average dollar loss statistics, and then some. They may have developed what we call "The Trader's Mindset" and possess superior trading psychology and confidence.

But, even the master will on occasion forget this very obvious fact that "not every trade will be a winner." This temporary amnesia might occur after a string of one substantially profitable trade after another. Even masters can fall prey to the illusion of being invincible every once in a while, and then they will be vulnerable to emotional trading.

We are all human, so no matter how expert we become, and no matter how fantastic our profits are, we need to remember the root of all trading evil—that is, the evil of forgetting to fully acknowledge and accept the risk of potential loss in every trade.

MAYBE, THE WORST THING THAT CAN HAPPEN IS TO HAVE A STREAK OF WINNERS IN THE VERY BEGINNING

It usually takes a while for the novice or beginner to fully appreciate the importance of recognizing that not all trades will be profitable and that they won't be right every time. Sometimes the worst thing that can happen to eager, and often very intelligent, investors entering the markets and making their first trades is to have a winning streak right from the start. Then they really believe all the infomercials that show you how to get rich quick.

As a beginner, they may be a little sloppy and may have poorly calculated their stops or have used no stops at all. They may have taken on far too much risk for their current portfolio size. The winning trades will, in effect, reward them for bad behavior and will give them the false sense of security that they know all there is to know about trading, and they are invincible.

You've seen all the disclaimers (including the one at the front of this book) that say "Past performance is not a guarantee of future results." That means if you have a few big winners, you are not "guaranteed" to have winners for the rest of your days.

The market is a living, breathing entity. It has ups and downs, bulls and bears, and if you get caught off guard, you can get a swift kick in the butt. So a word of caution to the novice traders reading this chapter: I want you to be profitable beyond your wildest dreams, but you must never let your guard down. Keep your eye on your money management.

THE TECH BUST KNOCKED OUT MANY NOVICE TRADERS

An example of having great success and then getting caught off guard happened to so many during the technology sector disaster that started in 2001.

There were many novice investors and traders that had made lots of "easy money" on the way up and then failed to realize when the market had changed. It financially killed a lot people who felt they were invincible, and it was the hole in their pocketbook that first made them realize that there is no such thing as being invincible in the markets.

If it happened to you, there is no shame. You are by no means alone. Friends of mine got hit by it, although I didn't even find out about their devastation until years later. To show you how having wins early on can be a bad thing, I want to share this story.

My friends started with a relatively small account of $50,000 in the year 1996. The husband was managing the account. By using leverage, he started making very profitable trades in the technology sector. The wins began to accumulate and the account grew quickly, doubled to $100,000, then doubled again to $200,000.

He had no real prior experience in the markets (the $50,000 was inheritance money), and the best investment this couple had made to that point was probably buying their home, which was accumulating terrific equity. So there was no real exit strategy in place for this $50,000 investment in the technology sector. Also, there was no real sector diversification in the portfolio. Probably, the thinking was, it can only go up, and if it goes down, we'll just get out. Which is certainly logical enough, right?

As the years went by, the exhilaration of generating such fantastic revenue (in addition to his regular "day job") was surely intoxicating, especially as the account grew to $500,000 and then to more than $1,000,000. The wife wanted to get her dream car, but the husband wanted to focus on building this "nest-egg" for their retirement and the kid's college fund. So he said, "Wait just a little longer honey. We'll get that car soon."

The end of the story is the technology market started to tank in the year 2001, and my friend was not emotionally ready to get out quick enough. There's the thinking, it can't go that much lower, I can't afford to get out now, and so on. So they lost the $1,000,000, plus the original $50,000. Now there is such despair and sadness after winning it all, and then losing it all, that they both are still feeling the agony of it seven years later.

The lesson to be learned is that your psychology is crucial, and sometimes winning big can cloud your rational judgment. Of course, losing big doesn't help either, so the goal is to keep an even keel emotionally during both the gains and the losses. Steady as she goes; don't focus on making an instant killing in your account, and work on consistent and steady growth in your equity curve. Consistency is what counts in this business.

PERFECTIONISTS BEWARE

If we now agree that every trade will not be a winner, how will the perfectionists reading this chapter be able to cope? If it means that there will be times that you are wrong, can you live with that?

We have a lot of clients that are fighter pilots, airline pilots, you name it. When we talk to them, it is interesting because they are the first to understand all the concepts of *paper trading* (just like flight simulators), following the trading rules (just like preflight checklist), and having discipline.

But the one thing these pilots have difficulty with is *stop-outs*. When you're 30,000 miles above land, there is no room for error (or stop-outs), or for being wrong, because when you are wrong it usually means you will crash and burn. They have little tolerance for imperfection.

So when they get stopped out, they have to rewire their thinking to remember that a stop-out is only a minor flight-plan course correction—it is not crashing and burning. Maybe a stop is the equivalent to turbulence that you eliminate by adjusting your altitude.

For the perfectionists, remember that stop-outs are a normal part of trading, and being wrong is not the end of the world, especially if you make the appropriate corrections in a timely manner. It is the big picture that matters at the end of the trading day, or week, or month, or year.

Progress counts, too. If you are losing $1000 a month right now because you are in the learning phase, when you reduce that monthly loss to $500 you better pat yourself on the back. Remember, any step toward greater profitability is a positive.

WHAT IS THE ANSWER?

If we are never going to get 100 percent perfection in our trades, then the answer to "How can we maintain profitability?" is the age-old adage of "cut your losses short and let your winners ride." That will require you to maintain discipline and adhere to eight guidelines:

1. Find a trading system or approach that is compatible with your personality, experience level, and comfort zone.

2. Paper trade (see Appendix C, The Art of Paper Trading, in this book) that system to determine what your win ratio and payoff ratio are (not what they are for the person that recommended the system to you). These statistics will be needed when you design your money

management system. You want to know how many dollars you earn for every dollar you lose and what your percentage of wins to losses is.

3. Always use a stop-loss exit to cut losses short, and base your stop on market dynamics rather than an arbitrary dollar amount.

4. Develop your psychology and confidence so that you consistently adhere to your stop-loss exits.

5. Determine proper trade size for your current portfolio size and limit your risk per trade to 2 percent. (Advanced traders, see important note following this list.)

6. Maintain impeccable records so you have a day-by-day analysis of your profit/loss performance, and know immediately when your system is failing due to a change in market cycle or in your psychology.

7. When your system is failing (by a given percentage that you have determined in your money management plan), stop trading with live money and go back to the drawing board (paper trading) to determine what the cause for failure is.

8. Once your testing and analysis and paper trading is proving profitable again, reenter the market with a live cash account.

IMPORTANT NOTE: For some advanced traders, it is beneficial to risk more than 2 percent of their trading account. The amount these traders risk must be carefully calculated depending on their proven historical performance statistics. See Chapter 9 for the formulas to determine if your payoff ratio and win ratio performance warrant a higher risk than 2 percent.

YOU'VE GOTTA HAVE A STOP

For our purposes, we will assume that you already have a system that tells you when to enter a trade. (See more about entry rules and trading systems in Chapter 6.)

After knowing where to enter, my first question is, does this system also tell you where to get out—*before* you enter the trade? My second question is, if you do have a system that tells you where to get out before you enter the trade, is this exit based on market dynamics? Meaning, are you taking into account market conditions that will tell you how much room you need to give your trade to "breathe" so that you don't get whipsawed and repeatedly stopped out?

On the road to profitability, let's agree that stop-loss exits are needed. Then we need to determine how to effectively select stop-loss exits to avoid excessive stop-outs. The more trades you place, the more commission fees you will pay, and the higher your costs of doing business will be. So right there you can increase your profitability if you increase the number of winning trades (your win ratio), thereby decreasing your commission expense.

This is not a book about developing a trading system, yet good money management is eternally linked to the system or approach you use. So, choose your system carefully, and be sure that your system is able to identify high-probability stop-loss exits that will reduce your number of stop-outs. The best way to do this is develop a stop-loss strategy that takes into account current market dynamics. (See more about stop-loss exits in Chapter 7.)

CHAPTER 6

Entry Rules and Your Trading System

F inding the right trading system or approach can be a lengthy process. It's a very personal choice, and it truly is like a relationship: There needs to be a connection and an understanding between you and your system. You must believe in your system and trust that it can produce consistent profits over time. Also, you have to understand that no system is perfect and no system can produce 100 percent winning trades.

If you have a system that isn't working for you, and your win ratio and payoff ratio don't generate a profit over time, then rethink your strategy. Make adjustments to the entries and exits, determine if it is your system that isn't working or is it your trading psychology that is off. See if the market cycle has changed. Maybe you need to adjust to the new market cycle.

Remember, to constantly jump from one system to another in search of the "holy grail" won't get you any closer to profitability if you don't give each system a chance to work. The decision to divorce your system should be a carefully thought out one, and you must be sure that you aren't merely afraid of commitment. Divorce of any kind can be emotionally and financially expensive, so proceed with caution.

FIND A SYSTEM THAT MAKES YOU FEEL COMFORTABLE AND CONFIDENT

Let's determine if you currently have a trading system in place. If you do not have a system, we will identify certain parameters to follow in selecting a system (see the sidebar). If you do currently have a system in place, review these parameters to see if your system needs adjustments.

The primary purpose of your system is to make you feel comfortable and confident—if you feel that way, you ultimately will also be profitable. You will feel this when your system has proven to you, and you have proven to it, that you can work together and generate consistent revenue. It is a team effort; you and your system are on the same team. Testing your system and working together will create a solid relationship between the two of you. After all, life is all about relationships, isn't it?

If you have not already done so, you need to paper trade your system to get the bugs out. For those readers with a system they have been using to make real trades in the markets, that will suffice. Determine what your personal win ratio and payoff ratio is using your system over time. These ratios will be used to develop a sound money management plan that will work hand in hand with your trading system.

It takes three to tango. That would be your trading system, your money management system, and *you*! The stronger and more developed the relationship is among the three of you, the more profitable you will be over time.

FIVE PARAMETERS TO FOLLOW WHEN SELECTING YOUR TRADING SYSTEM

The money management techniques presented in this book will work on any type of system, whether it be fundamental, technical, or a combination of the two. However, five parameters must be met in your system for these techniques to work:

1. Trade entries are defined based on market price activity, key support and resistance levels, volume, volatility dynamics, and/or fundamental rules (not on random and spontaneous decisions).

2. Actual initial stop-loss exit is determined *prior* to placing the trade.

3. Trade exit is based on market price activity, key support and resistance levels, volume, volatility dynamics, and/or fundamental rules, not on an arbitrary dollar loss that feels comfortable to you.

4. Your system has been adequately paper traded or live traded so that you have determined your personal statistical performance. You need to know your win ratio and payoff ratio. (Do not rely on the performance stated by others but the actual results you attain. Also, do not rely on computer back-testing results, as your personal performance results are the only

real results that matter. Back testing does not account for your trading psychology.)

5. Your trading system rules must be written out one by one so that entries and exits are consistent, clear, and quantifiable.

YOU KNOW WHERE TO GET IN—BUT WHERE AND WHEN DO YOU GET OUT?

Knowing where to get into a trade is just the beginning. Then there is the important task of knowing where to get out. From a money management standpoint, this exit decision must be made prior to placing the trade. With the entry and exit information, you can then mathematically calculate what your trade size will be, which will control your risk.

From a psychological standpoint, this exit decision must also be made prior to placing the trade. By identifying your initial stop-loss exit prior to the event, you reduce your chances of emotional trading, which can lead to disaster. Knowing that you need to determine your initial stop-loss exit before you enter a trade is going to put you leaps and bounds ahead of the average active trader. The next question is, do you know how to decide *where* and *when* to get out?

There are a variety of stop-loss exit strategies that you can use in determining your exit. My one word of caution is that you must be sure *not* to say, "I'll get out when the trade goes one point against me," or "When I lose $200.00 on this trade, then I'm out." These are random exit choices and are not based on constantly changing market dynamics and realities. So, whatever trading system you are using, be sure to design an exit strategy that takes into account current market dynamics.

ABOUT THE *ART*® TRADING SYSTEM

For the purposes of illustrating certain concepts, my examples will be based on entries and exits that have been identified by the *ART*®, also known as the *Applied Reality Trading* system. This is the system that I use, and it will easily provide clarity to the entry and exit strategies that we'll be discussing.

You do not need to use the *ART* system to use these money management techniques. Your primary goal is to understand the theory and adapt it to work with your system. System selection is a very personal thing, and it is crucial that you are working with a system in which you have confidence.

If you have not followed the five parameters (see sidebar) with your current system, you will need to do so. These five parameters are intended to ensure that you are trading in accordance with a plan as opposed to making random entry and exit choices, and to ensure that the plan has been tested to some degree so that you have proven to yourself that it works for you. Knowing that it works will go a long way in giving you confidence in your plan.

ART GIVES ME ENTRY AND EXIT SIGNALS BASED ON CURRENT MARKET DYNAMICS AND MARKET REALITIES

Just to give you a little background on the system I use, *Applied Reality Trading*, we're going to show you a few charts and cover the basic theory of the system. Then you will have a clear understanding of what I mean by choosing entries and exits based on *current market dynamics* and *realities*.

Let's look at the bullish trending chart in Figure 6.1. In this figure, you will see four bullish triangles (to the right of the chart) marked with a P.

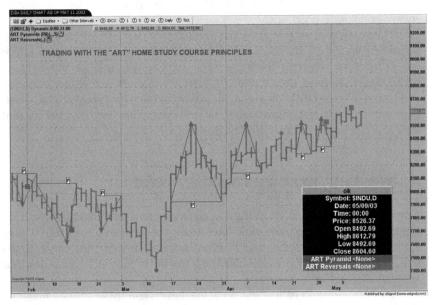

FIGURE 6.1 The *ART* Trading System Identifies Entries and Exits Based on Market Dynamics
Source: eSignal. www.eSignal.com

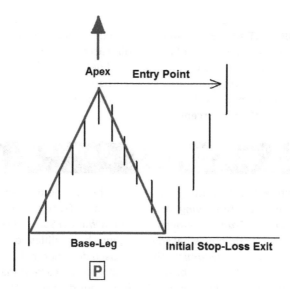

FIGURE 6.2 The *Bullish Pyramid Trading Point*® Signal Tells You Where to Enter and Where Your Initial Stop-Loss Exit Is
Source: eSignal. www.eSignal.com

The triangles are pointing in the upward direction, indicating a bullish trend. The P signal indicates a *primary* pyramid trading point that tells me these are high-probability entry and exit signals available to me if I choose to take them.

The entry will be taken one tick above the Apex of the first bullish triangle (the top) and the initial stop-loss exit will be taken one tick below the base of the first bullish triangle (the bottom). See Figure 6.2 for an illustration on how this works. Both of these signals are completely based on the current dynamics—and the realities—of the market and will give my trade the room it needs to "breathe" so that there is less chance of my trade being unnecessarily stopped out.

Now, my *trade risk* is going to be determined by measuring the distance between the Apex of the triangle and the base of the triangle. The dollar amount of the distance between the entry and the exit will determine my trade risk. So, with this information, and using my money management rules, I can calculate what my trade size should be in contracts or shares.

We'll cover this topic in Chapter 10, where you'll see how to best calculate your trade size based on what your trade risk is. Your *trade size* will be calculated by looking at the total number of dollars in your trading account and by risking no more than 2 percent of your total trading account capital on this one trade.

IMPORTANT NOTE: For some advanced traders, it is beneficial to risk more than 2 percent of their trading account. The amount these traders risk must be carefully calculated depending on their proven historical performance statistics. See Chapter 9 for the formulas to determine if your payoff ratio and win ratio performance warrant a higher risk than 2 percent.

The ART of Trading, A BOOK PUBLISHED BY JOHN WILEY & SONS

If you are interested in getting more information on the trading system I use, which is *Applied Reality Trading*, or *ART*, you can refer to the book that I wrote titled *The ART® of Trading*, published by John Wiley & Sons, 2008.

The *ART* methodology is based on trading the "realities" of the market, or trading *current market dynamics*. This approach does not try to predict or forecast the markets. Instead, it is based on looking at the current market realities, which are based on the data you receive from your data provider.

These realities of price and volume cannot be distorted. They are absolute in any given moment. By using this information, we can determine entries and exits based on the realities of current market conditions. We are then not relying on news, indicators, or opinions.

This book, *The ART of Trading,* is a thorough manual on technical analysis and how to use the *ART* trading system. Included with the purchase price of the book is one free month of the *ART* trading software and one free month of data feed from a major data supplier. Probably the best price for the book is on Amazon.com, so you can go online to see what the particulars are. If you have any questions on the *ART* system, feel free to contact me by e-mail via team@traderscoach.com.

ADAPTING TO CHANGING ENVIRONMENTS AND CHANGING MARKET CYCLES

Just as most climates have four seasons to one degree or another, the markets have different environmental cycles. This means you need to quickly identify the changing cycles and then appropriately adapt to them.

If you live in New York City, for example, chances are you will not be going outside for a leisurely stroll down Fifth Avenue in shorts and a tee shirt in the month of February. Why is that? Because, if you've lived there for a while, and experienced the local seasons, you will have already identified that February is pretty darn cold, and to appropriately adapt you will want to wear a winter coat and maybe gloves and ear muffs.

It is the same with the markets. You need to "live there for a while" and experience a variety of market cycles so you know what to wear, or rather how to adapt, so that you are financially comfortable. Instead of knowing to wear a winter coat in February you will know that in a choppy, sideways, bracketed market you need to adapt your system and rules so that you do not get whipsawed and stopped out a lot. Or, you may need to recognize a bull market changing to a bear market.

This is not a money management issue, but it is important in terms of your profitability and will work in conjunction with your money management. So, in addition to having a trading system you feel comfortable with, you need to learn what the different market cycles are. Then you need to learn how to correctly identify when the different market cycles are occurring.

Finally, you need to learn how to adapt your approach to those cycles to remain profitable. Effectively identifying market cycles is a skill that all successful traders have mastered.

FOUR MAJOR MARKET CYCLES

There are four major market cycles. Each market cycle requires a different approach from your trading system, and adapting to market cycles can improve your profitability dramatically:

1. **Trending.** A market is moving consistently in one direction, up or down. (See Figure 6.3, which shows a bullish trend in crude oil.)

2. **Consolidating.** Also known as bracketing, this is when the market is stuck in a price range between an identifiable *resistance* and *support* level. On a chart, it will look like a sideways horizontal line. (See Figure 6.4, which shows a bracketed e-mini market. Notice how the triangles, potential pyramid trading points, tell you this is a bracketing market when they form directly next to each other in a "down" "up" "down" "up" sideways pattern.)

3. **Breaking out of a consolidation.** There is a sharp change in price movement after the market has been consolidating for at least 20 price bars. (See Figure 6.5, which shows the bracketed e-mini market you saw in Figure 6.4 break out to the down side. Notice how the two "down" pyramid trading point triangles from Figure 6.4 were confirmed and the two "up" triangles disappeared.)

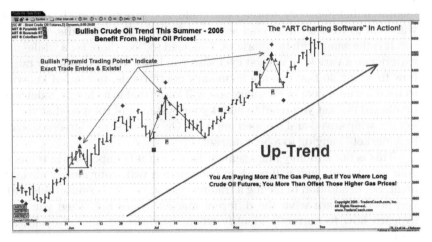

FIGURE 6.3 The *ART* Software Identifies a Trending Market
Source: eSignal. www.eSignal.com

4. **Corrective.** This is a short, sharp reverse in prices during a longer market trend. (See Figure 6.6, which shows you the bearish trend in the e-mini indicated by the P pyramid trading point triangles, which are all facing down. Notice the two corrections in this trend indicated

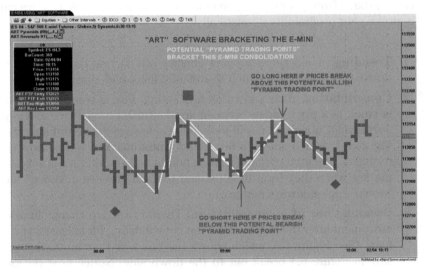

FIGURE 6.4 The *ART* Software Identifies a Consolidating Market
Source: eSignal. www.eSignal.com

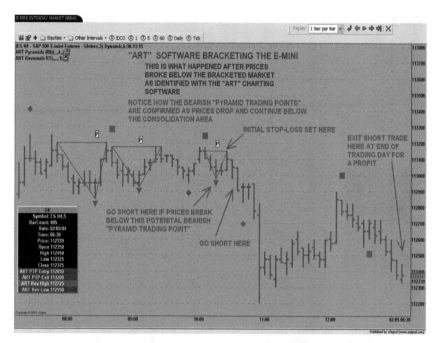

FIGURE 6.5 The *ART* Software Identifies a Market Breaking Out of a Consolidation
Source: eSignal. www.eSignal.com

by the MP, minor pyramid trading point triangles, facing "up," which indicates only a *correction* in the trend, *not* a change in trend yet.)

In addition to these four cycles, many traders also use Elliott wave theory to determine *waves*, which are also an indication of market cycles. There are five waves, and each has its own relevance in determining your trading strategy. Using Elliott waves is an advanced technique and requires that you have a thorough understanding and ability to correctly determine which wave your market is in.

Incorrectly identifying a market cycle—with either the four major cycles we've listed or by using Elliott wave theory—can be a costly situation. For example, if you incorrectly determined that a market entered a new trend, but in fact it was consolidating, you might enter a trend trade and immediately get stopped out. For this reason, market experience is the best teacher. Your best plan of action is constant observation. With that, you will continually improve your ability to read market cycles.

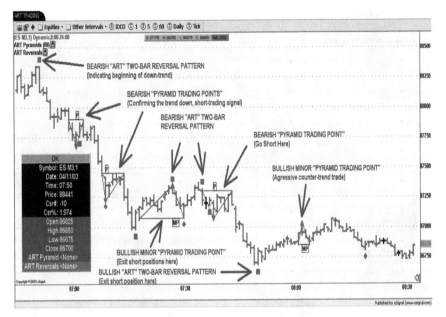

FIGURE 6.6 The *ART* Software Identifies a Market Correction with MP, minor pyramid trading point triangles.
Source: eSignal. www.eSignal.com

Remember, the "right side of the chart" is always an unknown quantity until it reveals itself. Hindsight is generally 20/20. Trying to predict the markets can be an elusive and impossible endeavor. So do not berate yourself if the ability to correctly identify market cycles takes you some time to develop.

YOUR TRADING SYSTEM IS YOUR BEST FRIEND

"A man's best friend is his dog," as the saying goes. In the markets, the trader's best friend is a sound trading system. If you take the time and energy to develop a winning system it will reward you with a lifetime of companionship and consistent profits.

CHAPTER 7

Stop-Loss Exit Rules

One important way to control your trading risk is by setting stop-loss exits. A stop-loss exit is a practical tool used in managing risk, and there is an art to developing the right strategy. On the one hand, you don't want to set stops that are so tight that you constantly get bumped out of the market. On the other hand, you don't want to be too liberal with your stops so that you never lock in profit.

The solution is to find an approach that is a balance of these two goals and is based on market dynamics. Your stop loss strategy should be designed to let your trade breathe and fluctuate with the normal ebb and flow of the market.

THERE'S A WORLD OF RISK IN TRADING: A RISK LIST TO LIVE BY

The value of having a stop-loss exit in place *prior* to entering the market is that you can unemotionally determine the best exit possible for the types of risk listed here. If you enter a trade before you think about where you are going to get out, you are dancing with the devil. Here's a *risk list* that your stop exits can help protect you from:

- **Trade risk**. The *calculated* risk you take on each individual trade is adjusted by changing your trade size. This is the only risk you can control. A good rule of thumb is to never risk more than 2 percent of the capital in your trading account on any one trade. (Advanced traders, see important note following this list.)

- **Market risk**. The *inherent* risk of being in the market is called market risk and we have absolutely no control over this type of risk. It includes the entire gamut of risk possible when in the markets. Market risk may cause your carefully calculated *trade risk* to be much larger than anticipated. Market risk can be far greater than *trade risk*. For this reason it is best that you never trade with more than 10 percent of your net worth. This type of risk encompasses catastrophic world events and market crashes that create complete paralysis in the markets. Events causing market *gaps* in price against your trade are also considered to be market risk.
- **Margin risk**. This involves risk where you can lose more than the dollar amount in your margined trading account. Because you are leveraged, you then *owe* the brokerage firm money if the trade goes against you.
- **Liquidity risk**. If there are no buyers when you want to sell, you will experience the inconvenience of liquidity risk. In addition to the inconvenience, this type of risk can be costly when the price is going straight down to zero and you are not able to get out, much like the experience of Enron shareholders in 2001. Liquidity risk can be caused by or aggravated by a *market risk* event.
- **Overnight risk**. For day traders, overnight risk presents a concern in that what can happen overnight, when the markets are closed, can dramatically impact the value of their position. There is the potential to have a *gap open* at the opening bell where the price is miles away from where it closed the day before. (See the sidebar "Rules of Engagement" later in this chapter for determining how to hold trades overnight.) This gap possibility can negatively impact your account value.
- **Volatility risk**. A bumpy market may tend to stop you out of trades repeatedly, creating significant drawdown. Volatility risk occurs when your stop-loss exits are not in alignment with the market and are not able to breathe with current price fluctuations.

IMPORTANT NOTE: For some advanced traders, it is beneficial to risk more than 2 percent of their trading account. The amount these traders risk must be carefully calculated depending on their proven historical performance statistics. See Chapter 9 for the formulas to determine if your payoff ratio and win ratio performance warrant a higher risk than 2 percent.

Risk is inevitable in the markets, and there is an art to managing the possibilities. It is not a matter of fearing the risk. Instead, focus on playing the "what-if" scenario so that you can adequately prepare yourself for any outcome.

SEVEN BASIC STOP-LOSS EXITS

The topic of where to set stop-loss exits generally falls under the heading of *trading system*. Your exits must be carefully coordinated with your entries, and this is a trading skill that must be developed with experience. The theory of stop selection is really a separate topic from money management, but they are so connected that it is important to give you an outline of stop theory as part of our discussion.

There are a variety of stops that you can incorporate into your system. The following seven are the ones I find most valuable:

1. **Initial stop.** First stop set at the beginning of your trade. This stop is identified before you enter the market. The initial stop is also used to calculate your position size. It is the largest loss you will take in the current trade. See Figure 7.1, where the first "up" triangle on the

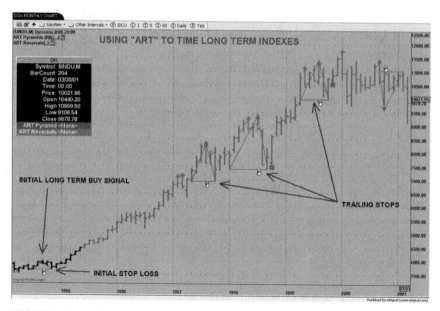

FIGURE 7.1 The *ART* Software Identifies the Initial Stop and the Subsequent Trailing Stops.
Source: eSignal. www.eSignal.com

bottom left-hand side of the chart is bullish and the initial stop is placed at the base leg of the pyramid trading point marked with a P.

2. **Trailing stop.** Develops as the market develops. This stop enables you to lock in profit as the market moves in your favor. See Figure 7.1, where the three up triangles marked P follow the initial stop loss that we set on the very first up triangle. These following three up triangles lock in profit as the bullish trend moves in our favor, and each stop is moved up to the base leg of each new up triangle. We exit the market when the market goes against us and our stop is hit on the up triangle in the upper-right corner of the chart.

3. **Resistance stop.** This is a form of trailing stop used in trends. It is placed just under countertrend pullbacks in a trend.

4. **Three-bar trailing stop.** This is used in a trend if the market seems to be losing momentum and you anticipate a reversal in trend.

5. **One-bar trailing stop.** When prices have reached your profit target zone, use this stop. You can also use it when you have a break-away market and want to lock in profits. Usually, use it after three to five price bars move strongly in your favor.

6. **Trend line stop.** Use a trend line placed under the lows in an uptrend or on top of the highs in a downtrend. You want to get out when prices close on the opposite side of the trend line. (See Figure 7.2.)

7. **Regression channel stop.** Use a regression channel to set your stops. Very similar to a regular trend line, but the regression channel forms a nice channel between the highs and lows of the trend and usually represents the width of the trend channel. Stops are placed outside the low of the channel on uptrends and outside the high of the channel in downtrends. Prices should close outside the channel for the stop to be taken. (See Figure 7.2.)

Other stop possibilities are usually derivatives of one of these seven stops. Setting stops will require judgment by you, the trader. Judgment is based on experience and the type of trader you are. You will set your stops based on your psychology and comfort level.

If you find you are getting stopped out too frequently, or if you seem to be getting out of trends too early, then chances are, you are trading from a fearful mindset. Try and let go of your fear and place stops at reasonable places in the market.

Position your stops in relation to market price activity; don't pick an arbitrary place to set your stop. Many traders incorrectly choose a stop so their loss is the same exact dollar amount each time they are stopped out. By doing this, they are completely disregarding the meaningful market support and resistance areas where stops should be set.

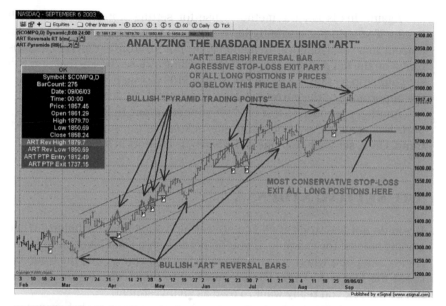

FIGURE 7.2 Illustration of a Trend Line Stop and a Regression Channel Stop.
Source: eSignal. www.eSignal.com

YOU CAN SET YOUR INITIAL STOP 3 PERCENT BEYOND SUPPORT

This is *not* a method that I personally use since my trade entries and exits are determined by the *ART* trading software, but this method does satisfy, to some degree, the need for placing stops at junctures relating to current market dynamics. The key with this method is to effectively identify meaningful support areas. Test this method and see if it works for you.

If your trading system has determined an entry point, but does not provide an exit based on market dynamics you would first identify an area of support. Then set your stop 3 percent away from the support. For example in an established bullish trend if you have an area of support at $26.89 you would set your stop three percent below that.

Formula:

$$\text{Support Price} \times 0.97 = \text{Initial Stop Loss Price}$$

Example:

$$\$26.89 \times 0.97 = \$26.08$$

Again, this is *not* the method I use for setting stops, but it is worth testing if you do not currently have a system that selects stops based on current market dynamics. Remember, do not arbitrarily determine stops based on the flat dollar amount you are willing to lose. To say that you will set your stop so that the most you lose is $100 or one point is to disregard the importance of the current market conditions.

Another approach to test is to set your stop "one tick" beyond the support. For example, set your stop one tick *below* the support in a bullish trend. On V, set your stop one tick *above* the support in a bearish trend.

NOT SETTING STOPS

If you do not use stops at all you are setting yourself up for failure. When trading stocks, for example, if you do not use stops and hang on to losing trades to a point where you emotionally feel you cannot exit the trade because the loss is so large, you are married to the stock. However, it may not be a stock you really want to own as an investment.

Some stocks we trade are good for short-term trades only because we are taking advantage of the momentum. It may be a stock we would never invest in and hold for a long time. If you find yourself wishing for a trade to turn around, you're not trading well. Based on the reasons you entered and the location of your stop, you should always know in a second whether you will be in or out.

SETTING MENTAL STOPS

For some markets, it is better not to put the stop actually in the market when you have the position on. Some market makers will see your stop, and if there are enough other traders with similar stops, the market makers may try and hit your stop. Then they make money and you do not.

In markets like this, you can set a mental stop and get out immediately if it is hit. Be sure you have the psychological toughness and discipline to get out when you are supposed to. If you don't, then go ahead and enter the stop when you take the trade.

MOVING STOPS

Never move your stop for emotional reasons, especially when it is your initial stop (see Figure 7.1). As new trailing stops are determined, you can move your stops to lock in profit. If you add on to your winning trade (increase your *trade size*), your stop must be adjusted to keep your risk in relation to your new trade size.

When adjusting your stop due to an increase in trade size, always move the stop closer to your current position to lower the risk in relation to your larger trade size. (An increase in trade size is usually caused by adding on or scaling in to a winning position.) Once you do this, you should never roll back your stop, since now your larger trade size will warrant the tighter stop to maintain proper risk control.

Many traders ask about moving stops based on different time frames. This is an advanced technique. As a general rule, always set your stops on the same time frame as you entered the trade. In other words, if you use a daily chart to base your trade entry, use the daily chart to set your initial stop.

There are exceptions to this, but only after you have developed enough experience. Become profitable using the same time frame first, and then perhaps venture into multiple time frames later.

RULES OF ENGAGEMENT FOR OVERNIGHT TRADES

For day traders, there is risk when holding trades overnight, since there is always a possibility of unforeseen events occurring after hours. Unexpected events can create a *gap open,* which may adversely affect your account value.

For example, if you were trading a 15-minute time frame, your stop loss and position size would be based on the 15-minute time frame. But, let's say you are five minutes from the close of the day and the trade is profitable and much more profit is possible if you hold the trade overnight based on your 15-minute chart.

When this happens, consider five rules:

1. The trade must currently be profitable.

2. The 15-minute chart must indicate a solid trend in place.

3. You must set a new stop-loss exit based on the *daily* chart.

4. Reduce your trade size so that risk remains no more than 2 percent of your trading account based on the new adjusted stop from the daily chart. (Advanced traders, see important note following this list.)

5. Be sure to monitor the trade at the opening bell when the market opens the next day.

In this way you will take into account the inherent risks of holding the trade overnight. This will not eliminate your risk, but it will reduce it.

IMPORTANT NOTE: For some advanced traders, it is beneficial to risk more than 2 percent of their trading account. The amount these traders risk must be carefully calculated depending on their proven historical performance statistics. See Chapter 9 for the formulas to determine if your payoff ratio and win ratio performance warrant a higher risk than 2 percent.

THE DOWN SIDE TO POORLY SELECTED STOP-LOSS EXITS

Having the discipline to set a stop-loss exit and adhere to it is better than not, even if it is a poorly selected stop. With that said, the better your stop strategy is, the more profitable you will be. So it is crucial from a revenue standpoint to refine your approach.

The most common down side to a less than perfect stop-loss exit is that you will get stopped out on the correction and then the market will race back in the direction you initially were betting on. Repeated stop-outs can also eat into your bottom line by racking up commission fees.

Keep in mind, there is no perfect stop and there is no way to time the market perfectly. Your goal is to get the probabilities to lean in your favor. With experience, you will incorporate a variety of live market lessons into your own approach. This experience is the key to increasing your profitability curve. But remember to always select your initial stop-loss exit prior to entering the market.

THE MARKET HAS TO BREATHE, AND SO DO YOUR STOPS

The market is a living, breathing thing, and it rarely goes entirely in only one direction for an extended period of time. Rather, it goes in one direction, has a correction, continues back in its trend direction, has another correction, and so on. It inhales and exhales, it goes up, it goes down, and you need to give it the freedom to do that. Even in a sideways market, there are ups and downs; it is like the ebb and flow of the tides, back and forth. It is nature, and you must learn to ebb and flow with it.

This is why setting stops on key levels of price support is crucial. Usually key support levels represent significant market realities occurring with enough trade volume to warrant a stop loss level.

Accepting the reality that the market will continually fluctuate, how do you reduce the possibility that you might get stopped out of a perfectly good trend by the normal ebb and flow of the market?

The answer lies in the current dynamics of the market as represented by price, volume, and volatility. You will need to be sure that your system and approach take these factors into consideration in a meaningful way so as to allow your stops to breathe with the market. They need to protect you from risk, yes, but at the same time they need to allow the market freedom to fluctuate.

USE CURRENT MARKET DYNAMICS TO DETERMINE YOUR STOP

One closing note on stop-loss exits is to remind you that whatever strategy you develop in choosing stop-loss exits, be sure that you do not use an arbitrary dollar amount like, "I'll get out of this trade when it goes against me $200," or "We'll set our stop loss so that we don't lose more than one or two points on this trade." To choose a random exit that does not include the crucial information the market is giving you at any given time is ignoring what the market is telling you. If you know how to listen to the market, it will tell you where to set your stop.

Identify the correct stop loss exit based on market dynamics. Then adjust your trade size to manage your dollar loss. Not the other way around.

CHAPTER 8

Scaling Out and Scaling In

T he technique of *scaling out* is a favorite of mine for reducing stress when the market has a quick turn in my favor. By taking just a small portion of my winning position off the table to lock in profit, I'm less likely to panic out of a trend that may still have a long way to go. Here again, the right side of the chart has an uncanny way of creating anxiety. Looking for a signal of some sort that tells me that it is a good time to scale out takes the randomness out of the decision process.

And of course *scaling in* is a great way to generate additional profit when your signals tell you that there is a strong trend in place. Here we'll talk about how to be sure you still keep your risk in line when you scale in, or add on, to a position. You've got to calculate the proper trade size so that you keep your risk percent in line.

SCALING OUT LOCKS IN PROFIT AND RELIEVES ANXIETY

Scaling out of trades is a technique that can convert some losing trades into profitable ones, reduce stress, and increase your bottom line. You can use *scaling out* techniques for *trend trading, scalping,* and *countertrend trading.* And it works on *all* time frames.

It is important to reduce stress while you're in a trade. Then you can focus on the trade and not be subject to emotions such as fear and greed.

Properly *scaling out* of positions can not only make you more profitable, but also significantly reduce stress.

In order to scale out of trades, your initial trade size must be large enough so you can reap the benefits of scaling out. The technique is applicable for both long and short positions, and for all markets—including futures, stocks, indexes, and options. The key is to initiate a large enough trade size while not risking more than 2 percent on entering the trade.

IMPORTANT NOTE: For some advanced traders, it is beneficial to risk more than 2 percent of their trading account. The amount these traders risk must be carefully calculated depending on their proven historical performance statistics. See Chapter 9 for the formulas to determine if your payoff ratio and win ratio performance warrant a higher risk than 2 percent.

When scaling out, your trade size, in contracts or shares, should be large enough so that you can take one-third of your position out of the market when you get a signal to do so. After taking your first third off the table, you can take one more third off if a second scaling signal presents itself. The remaining third stays on until your stop-loss exit is hit.

Take a look at Figure 8.1, which shows a bearish trend and six consecutive bearish primary pyramid trading points labeled with a P. This is a strong profitable trend. Statistically, the *ART* trading system exhibits *trend exhaustion* after four to five consecutive pyramid trading points in the same direction.

What this tells me is that by the fourth down triangle, the trend is probably nearing exhaustion. Given my entry and exit rules, I have not been stopped out on this trade yet, but at the same time it is clear that due to trend exhaustion, it may be time to scale out a portion of my position.

So, when a bullish *ART* reversal presents itself, that signal tells me there is an opportunity to scale-out of 30 percent of my position and I do so. The market meanders along sideways, and another bullish *ART* reversal presents itself. Again, I liquidate another 30 percent of my position. The remaining portion stays on until I am stopped out as price activity heads north.

Figure 8.2 shows another example of this scaling-out technique. Here, this bull market experiences a hyperbolic move to the upside, which always has a way of getting my attention. In this example, you will see three consecutive up triangles labeled with a P prior to the hyperbolic move.

At the top of this sharp upturn is a down triangle labeled with an MP, which is a minor pyramid trading point. This signal does not indicate a trend change; it only indicates a trend correction. The MP signal is the one

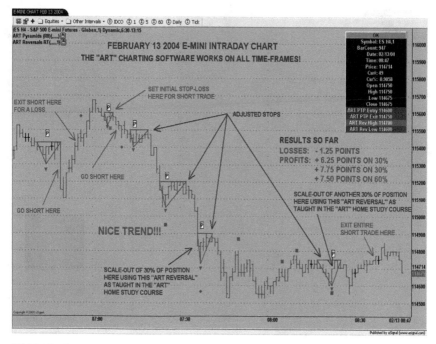

FIGURE 8.1 Scaling Out of a Trend to Lock in Profit When My System Tells Me There Is A High Probability That The Trend Is Nearing Exhaustion.
Source: eSignal.www.eSignal.com

I use to scale out of first 30 percent of this position. A bearish *ART* reversal appears, and I take the second 30 percent off the table. The remaining 40 percent of my position stays on until price activity triggers the stop exit.

Figures 8.1 and 8.2 give you an idea of how scaling out can be like an insurance policy to lock in profit. It's a terrific technique that can be used in a variety of ways, and you can test your own approach to see what works best for you.

TWO WAYS TO INCREASE YOUR TRADE SIZE AND MAINTAIN SOLID RISK CONTROL

Given that you need to have a large enough trade size to warrant scaling out, it is clear that trading only one contract would not enable you to scale out. You need to have at least three contracts to use this technique

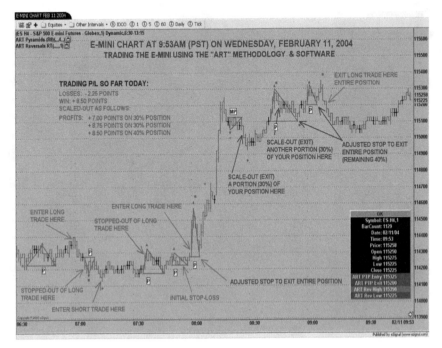

FIGURE 8.2 Scaling out of a Trend to Lock in Profit After A Quick Hyperbolic Market Move Up.
Source: eSignal.www.eSignal.com

effectively. In addition to having a large enough trade size, you also need to keep your trade risk below 2 percent.

IMPORTANT NOTE: For some advanced traders, it is beneficial to risk more than 2 percent of their trading account. The amount these traders risk must be carefully calculated depending on their proven historical performance statistics. See Chapter 9 for the formulas to determine if your payoff ratio and win ratio performance warrant a higher risk than 2 percent.

The two ways you can increase your trade size while maintaining solid risk control are as follows:

1. Find a market where you can initiate a large enough trade size with your current trading account capital while risking no more than 2 percent if this initial position is stopped out. This would mean finding markets that are less expensive and that therefore enable you to buy more contracts or shares.

2. Add additional trading capital to your trading account to allow for a larger position while still keeping risk within 2 percent.

Another alternative is to use the leverage of options, but you must be familiar with options, their time value decay, delta, and so on. Using options would be considered a specialty or advanced technique, and if you are not familiar with them, this method could lead to increasing your stress and your potential risk.

SCALING OUT EXAMPLE ON THE E-MINI

Using the e-mini as an example, your account size is $25,000 and you choose to risk 2 percent on this trade; 2 percent of $25,000 is $500. Your trade entry is 1037.75 and your exit is 1036.25, so you can buy approximately six contracts and stay within your risk parameters. (In this example, we are risking 1.5 points per contract, which is valued at $50 per point.) If you get stopped out before having a chance to scale out, your loss would only be 2 percent. Therefore, this potential risk should not create any stress.

Only when your trade becomes profitable does scaling out come into play. At the point your trade becomes significantly profitable, cover part of the position and liquidate enough contracts so that if you are then stopped out, you will still make a profit. If the trade becomes even more profitable and you have a large enough trade size, then you may want to liquidate another portion of contracts to lock in additional profit. The remaining portion of your position should stay in place.

Until you get stopped out, you should be able to enjoy the rest of the trade and let it go as long as the trend continues, knowing that no matter what happens, at the very least you will make a profit on this trade. Look at your trading system to determine if there is some type of reversal signal that will tell you when to scale out. Work some rules into the plan so that your decision to scale out is based on a technical or fundamental signal of some type.

When trading only one or two contracts, you can't scale out of positions in a meaningful way. This is another reason why larger trading accounts have an advantage over smaller ones. Also, some markets are more expensive than others, so the cost of the shares or contracts will determine your trade size.

Remember that in choosing your market, liquidity is important, and you must have sufficient market liquidity to successfully scale out of positions. Poor fills due to poor liquidity can adversely affect this technique.

The psychology of scaling out is to reduce stress by locking in profit, which should help you stay in trends longer with your remaining positions.

SCALING IN TO A POSITION AND INCREASING TRADE SIZE

Since this is a book on money management and risk control, it is appropriate to discuss how to control risk on a popular strategy of adding onto trends to increase your trade size with the goal of increasing profits. This technique is called *scaling in* or *adding on* to a trade in progress and is usually used in *trend trading*.

The basics are to increase your trade size on an already profitable trade while maintaining strict risk control throughout the trade. The reason for scaling in to a trend is to gain more profit through a larger trade size. It is important to distinguish scaling in from another technique known as *doubling down*, which is a form of adding to your trade size. Unfortunately, doubling down also increases your trade risk.

With doubling down, you add to your trade size when the trade goes against you and your open trade is currently at a loss. By adding to your position at a time when your position is losing, you are increasing your trade size and lowering your cost basis. However, you are also increasing your trade risk since the new added-on position will assume risk in addition to the risk of your initial open trade. Thus, you have an increase in the overall risk of your trade. For this reason, doubling down can be a loser's game, since your risk increases beyond the risk-of-ruin percentage guidelines used to carefully calculate your trade size, which determines your trade risk on the initial position.

A better way to add on to your current position is to add on *only* when your stop loss on your initial trade size moves to a price level where there is no longer any trade risk. This means that if you are stopped out, your initial trade is either a break-even trade or a profitable one. Moving your stop loss in this fashion is called a *trailing stop*.

Thus, when you are adding on or scaling in to a trade using this technique, you are not incurring additional trade risk since your new trailing stop loss nullifies the risk assumed from the initial position taken. When scaling in, you scale in with a trade size that is, again, carefully calculated so that your add-on position has a trade size that is within the risk-of-ruin guidelines. After scaling in, your new overall trade risk is the risk of the add on only.

A final word of caution needs to be mentioned in regards to scaling in or adding on to any position. Although we can control *trade risk* by carefully calculating trade size, we cannot control *market risk*. Trade risk is the risk we assume based on set stop-losses and proper trade size. Market risk is unforeseen events that cause market gaps and bad stop-loss fills that can offset the predetermined trade risk we planned for. Because of market risk, always trade with risk capital, and be careful of your overall portfolio risk.

Trade Size
Does Matter

CHAPTER 9

Using Risk-of-Ruin Tables and the Optimal *f* Formula

Y ou can effectively use the *risk-of-ruin principle* to significantly improve your bottom line. What you will learn about in this chapter is how to control the percent of capital you risk on each trade so that your have a minimal chance of being ruined.

There are a number of ways to calculate the percent of capital you should risk, all of which require that you know what your current win ratio and payoff ratio are. So, for starters, if you don't already know what those numbers are, you need to put that project at the top of your to do list. (See Chapter 11 to learn more about how to calculate these numbers.)

YOUR SURVIVAL DEPENDS ON HAVING RESPECT FOR THE RISK OF RUIN

Risk of ruin (ROR) has been extensively studied by mathematicians and by traders, and is the basis for most money management systems. The theory is based on a formula that will tell you what the chances are that you, given a historical win ratio and payoff ratio, are likely to go completely bankrupt and to be ruined.

Ideally you want to design a money management system that will protect you from ruin and will give you 0 percent likely (this is not guarantee) chance of going completely bankrupt. The ROR mathematical formula is based on three components:

1. **Win ratio.** This is based on your percentage of wins and your probability of winning. For example, if your win ratio is 40 percent, you have 40 percent wining trades and 60 percent losing trades.

2. **Payoff ratio.** Average winning trade dollar amount divided by the average losing trade dollar amount. This is how many dollars you earn compared to one dollar lost—for example, 3 to 1 would mean you earn three dollars for every one dollar you lose.

3. **Percent of capital exposed to trading.** If you are a novice trader it is recommended that you risk no more than 2 percent of your trading account value on any one trade. Otherwise, you can determine the optimal percent of capital to risk by either referring to a risk-of-ruin table (see Nauzer Balsara's book, *Money Management Strategies for Futures Traders*, or Tushar Chande's book, *Beyond Technical Analysis, 2nd ed.*) or by using the optimal *f* formula in this chapter.

Your trading system design and your skills as a trader govern the first two items in the risk of ruin, and your money management system controls the third item. The risk of ruin potential decreases as the payoff ratio increases or the probability of winning increases. The larger the percent of capital risked on each trade, the higher the chances for risk of ruin.

IMPORTANT NOTE: For some advanced traders, it is beneficial to risk more than 2 percent of their trading account. The amount these traders risk must be carefully calculated depending on their proven historical performance statistics. See the formulas in this chapter to determine if your payoff ratio and win ratio performance warrant a higher risk than 2 percent.

For our purposes, we are assuming that you already have a system that gives you an edge and provides you with a payoff ratio that is better than 1 to 1. You can estimate what your probabilities of ruin are by identifying what your payoff ratio and win ratio are and by referring to the risk-of-ruin tables found in Tushar Chande's book and also Nauzer Balsara's:

Tushar Chande, *Beyond Technical Analysis, 2nd ed.*, John Wiley & Sons, 2001, has the following risk-of-ruin tables:

- 1 percent capital at risk
- 1.5 percent capital at risk
- 2 percent capital at risk

Nauzer Balsara, *Money Management Strategies for Futures Traders,* John Wiley & Sons, 1992, has the following risk-of-ruin tables:

- 10 percent capital at risk
- 20 percent capital at risk
- 25 percent capital at risk
- 33.33 percent capital at risk
- 50 percent capital at risk
- 100 percent capital at risk

A small portion of Balsara's 10 percent risk-of-ruin table (see Table 9.1) is included in this chapter, with the author's permission. By far, Balsara's risk-of-ruin tables are the most comprehensive you will find. His book is an essential reference for determining your risk exposure based on your win ratio and payoff ratio.

It is quite revealing to see how your probabilities in these tables can go from 100.0 percent likely chance of ruin to 0.0 percent. So with a little planning and thought, you can dramatically increase your odds of survival just by having respect for the ROR formula. You do not need to be a mathematical genius and you don't need to know how to do the calculations yourself, just understand the principles and the impact that your risk choices make.

Keeping in mind that the past does not necessarily predict the future, it is imperative that you constantly monitor your current win ratios and

TABLE 9.1 Risk of Ruin (ROR) Probabilities with 10% of Capital at Risk

Risk of Ruin Probabilities with 10% of Capital at Risk	Payoff Ratio 1 To 1	Payoff Ratio 2 To 1	Payoff Ratio 3 To 1	Payoff Ratio 4 To 1	Payoff Ratio 5 To 1
Win Ratio 25%	100.0%	100.0%	99.0%	30.3%	16.2%
Win Ratio 30%	100.0%	100.0%	27.7%	10.2%	6.0%
Win Ratio 35%	100.0%	60.8%	8.2%	3.6%	2.3%
Win Ratio 40%	100.0%	14.3%	2.5%	1.3%	0.8%
Win Ratio 45%	100.0%	3.3%	0.8%	0.4%	0.3%
Win Ratio 50%	99.0%	0.8%	0.2%	0.1%	0.1%
Win Ratio 55%	13.2%	0.2%	0.1%	0.1%	0.0%
Win Ratio 60%	1.7%	0.0%	0.0%	0.0%	0.0%

A 0.0% probability means the total loss of equity is unlikely, but not impossible.

Source: The calculations on this table were prepared by Professor Nauzer Balsara. For additional calculations and reference tables on the risk of ruin, refer to his book, *Money Management Strategies for Futures Traders*, John Wiley & Sons, 1992, starting on page 18. This book has, by far, the most extensive set of ROR tables and formulas available.

payoff ratios to adjust the percentage of risk you take with every new trade. Use the formulas you will find in Chapter 11 of this book to calculate your win ratios and payoff ratios.

Since your payoff ratio and probability of winning are not constant, and these numbers will change daily, you will need to adjust your risk percentage accordingly. Determining how to analyze this data in and of itself can be a part of your personal money management plan.

PROFESSOR NAUZER BALSARA WROTE THE BOOK ON THE RISK OF RUIN TABLES

If you want the most extensive and comprehensive book on ROR tables, you must get *Money Management Strategies for Futures Traders* by Nauzer Balsara, John Wiley & Sons, 1992. This book is essential and required reading for any serious trader and has a wealth of information for all traders, not just futures traders. Amazon. com no doubt has the best price, and it is well worth the investment.

In this book, starting on page 18, you will find a complete set of ROR tables. The parameters covered include payoff ratios of 1, 2, 3, 4, 5, 6, 7, 8, 9, and 10. It includes win ratios from 5 percent wins all the way up to 90 percent wins. There is a table for 10 percent risked capital up to 100 percent risked capital.

Truly, this information will arm you with the statistical data you need to risk the correct amount as your payoff ratio increases from 1 to 2 to 3, and so on. Remember, it is crucial to recalculate your risk amount for each trade based on your current performance ratios.

RUNNING THE NUMBERS

Now that we've defined what the risk of ruin possibilities are, we need to know what our personal rate of return is on our current system. Again, we are assuming that you already have a trading system in place and that the system over time is producing for you a better than 1-to-1 payoff ratio. Meaning, you are making a profit instead of breaking even or incurring losses over time.

This means that you must be tracking your trades, and determining what your win ratio is and what your payoff ratio is. If you are not currently doing this, then start now so that you can obtain historical data. It may be helpful, if you have access to your old trading records, to go back in time and determine what these statistics are—basically, *run the numbers*.

You will find blank trade posting cards and ledgers that will be useful for this purpose in Appendix B. For details on how to use these forms see Chapter 13, which shows you how to calculate the statistics you will need.

AFTER YOU RUN THE NUMBERS

After you run the numbers on your current rate of return, you will need to evaluate what percent of your trading account should be risked on each trade to avoid the risk of ruin. Here are four hypothetical trading scenarios using a risk amount of 2 percent of your trading account on each trade (the following risk of ruin calculations for a 2, 1.5, and 1 percent risk amount come from Tushar Chande's book, *Beyond Technical Analysis*, 2nd ed., page 288):

1. **Win ratio 45 percent, payoff ratio 1 to 1, with 2 percent at risk, ROR probability is 100 percent.** In this case, you could reduce the percent of capital risked from 2 percent to 1 percent and your ROR probability would change from 100.0 percent likely chance of ruin to 52.4 percent—almost half. Your next goal would be to review your trading system to improve your payoff ratio to at least 1.5 which would bring your probability of ruin to 0.

2. **Win ratio 35 percent, payoff ratio 2 to 1, with 2 percent at risk, ROR probability is 16 percent.** This example shows more stable numbers than the first example so just by reducing the percent of capital risked from 2 percent to 1 percent on each trade your ROR probability would change from 16.0 percent to 0.1 percent—nearly 0.

3. **Win ratio 25 percent, payoff ratio 3 to 1, with 2 percent at risk, ROR probability is 19.7 percent.** Here, your win ratio is too low, and your first goal is to raise it to 30 percent, which would allow you to risk 2 percent of your capital on each trade and would reduce your ROR probability to 0.0 percent.

4. **Win ratio 50 percent, payoff ratio 3 to 1, with 2 percent at risk ROR probability is 0.0 percent.** These are statistics of an advanced trader, and as such you could risk 10 percent of your trading account on a trade and maintain a 0.2 percent risk of ruin (see Table 9.1). Remember, when you reach this level, be sure to reduce your trade size if your performance statistics dramatically change. For example, if your win ratio drops to 35 percent, be sure to adjust the percentage of your account you have at risk.

These four examples give you a start and show you how to use the grids in the ROR tables to learn where you want to focus your energy to keep you in the game. (Also use example 4 to recognize when you have reached the advanced trader level.)

Sometimes getting risk in line is as easy as reducing the percent of risk you take on each trade and sometimes you need to focus on your win ratio and the number of winning trades you have. Also, giving attention to your exit points may enable you to significantly improve your payoff ratio. If you are a trend trader, just staying in a profitable trend longer can boost your bottom line. Get creative and let the math create motivation and see where it leads you.

OPTIMAL *f* FORMULA CALCULATES THE OPTIMAL FRACTION OF CAPITAL TO BE RISKED

This formula was originally developed by John L. Kelly Jr. of Bell Labs in the early 1940s, and is sometimes referred to as the *Kelly formula*. Edward O. Thorp in *The Mathematics of Gambling* modified the fixed-fraction formula to account for the average payoff ratio, *A*, in addition to the average probability of success, *p*. The figures you will calculate using this formula are more aggressive than using the risk of ruin tables.

In his book *Money Management Strategies for Futures Traders*, Professor Nauzer J. Balsara defines the formula for determining the optimal fraction, *f*, of capital to be risked on a trade as follows:

$$f = \frac{[(A+1) \times p] - 1}{A}$$

In this formula, the following definitions apply:

- *f* is the optimal fraction (percentage) to be risked on one trade.
- *A* is the average payoff ratio. (dollars earned to one dollar lost).
- *p* is the average win ratio (probability in percentage of success).

Here is an example of the formula in use:

- *f* is the unknown quantity (of the optimal percentage to be risked).
- *A* is an average payoff ratio of 2 to 1.
- *p* is an average win ratio of 35 percent winning trades.

$$f = \frac{[(2+1) \times 0.35] - 1}{2} = \frac{1.05 - 1}{2} = \frac{.05}{2} = .025$$

To get a percentage, multiply *f* result by 100.

This gives a value of .025 for f, or 2.5 percent is the optimal percentage of your trading account to risk on a trade based on this performance data and the optimal f formula.

COMPARING OPTIMAL f EQUATION RESULTS TO THE RISK-OF-RUIN TABLES

Optimal f equation results give you a higher risk percentage than the risk-of-ruin tables do when striving for a 0 percent likely chance of ruin. Let's look at the following example:

- f is the unknown quantity (the optimal percentage to be risked).
- A is an average payoff ratio of 2 to 1.
- p is an average win ratio of 40 percent winning trades.

The equation looks like this:

$$f = \frac{[(2+1) \times 0.40] - 1}{2} = \frac{1.2 - 1}{2} = \frac{.2}{2} = .10$$

In this example, the optimal f formula calculates that for a trader with a payoff ratio of 2 to 1 and a win ratio of 40 percent winning trades, the optimal amount of capital to risk is 10 percent. When we refer to Table 9.1 we see Balsara's calculation for this scenario gives us a risk-of-ruin probability of 14.3 percent, which is a small risk but *not* a zero probable risk.

Using the optimal f formula, you should understand that it does not calculate a risk percentage that gives you a 0 percent probability of ruin. It is a more aggressive approach than when using the ROR tables. When using the ROR tables you can select a percent to risk that gives you a 0 percent probability of ruin.

ACCOUNT DRAWDOWN

Having equity drawdown in trading is normal, and drawdown is what causes the novice trader to be ruined because the novice trader has not yet learned the art of stop-loss exits, position sizing, and controlling the percent of their account that is risked on each trade.

Drawdown can be the result of a series of consecutive losses or from one loss. It is important to record historical data when trading your system to determine the following:

- Largest account drawdown in percentage. This is the largest percent of equity lost in a drawdown. It tells you your worst-case scenario and can be used to help predict the highest future loss.
- Largest account drawdown in dollars. This gives you a handle on actual dollars you can lose during drawdown.
- Largest number of consecutive losses. Historically, what is the maximum number of losses in a row? This figure can be used to estimate future drawdown events. For example, if your system has a maximum number of five losses in a row and you are risking 2 percent on each trade, your total maximum drawdown would be approximately 10 percent of your trading account. If you know this is normal, you will continue trading. Statistically, you are likely to benefit from winning trades following the drawdown.

The psychological impact of drawdown can be significant. This is where self-doubt and ego come into play. This is when you will be tested and will develop "The Trader's Mindset."

CHAPTER 10

Using the Two Percent Risk Formula and Proper Trade Size Formula

E ffective risk control requires that you do a little math and learn a few equations. In the last chapter you learned about the risk-of-ruin tables and using the optimal f equation to find out what the best percent of capital is to risk on any one trade. In this chapter, we're going to cover a few more equations to help you determine the right trade size to keep your risk in line.

WHEN CONTROLLING RISK, THERE ARE THREE VARIABLES YOU CAN PLAN TO CONTROL

1. Entry (where to get in)
2. Exit (where to get out—be sure to take into account market liquidity)
3. Size (in shares or contracts)

IT'S A NUMBERS GAME

Money management is all about numbers and probabilities, and the difference between being a winning trader and being a losing trader sometimes comes down to a few simple equations.

In this book you've seen how the risk-of-ruin tables, win ratio, payoff ratio, and percent of capital at risk determine if you are in danger of losing it all. The good news is that you can adjust these factors to work in your

favor, and it is not all that hard to do. The first priority is to correctly identify what needs to be adjusted, so you know where to focus your energy.
Three very important formulas enable you to control risk:

1. 2 percent risk formula
2. Trade size formula
3. Trade size formula using leverage

TWO PERCENT RISK FORMULA

As a starting point, I recommend that you do not risk more than 2 percent on any one individual trade. If you are a more advanced trader and
choose to risk more than 2 percent, you will want to substitute the 2 percent amount in this formula with the percent you decide to have at risk
prior to doing this calculation.

Formula: Account size × 2% = Risk amount

Example: $25,000 × 2% = $500

Remember, the risk amount of $500 includes commission and slippage,
so as you will see in the following trade size example, you will need to take
that into account. Now that you know what amount you will risk on your
trade ($500) you can figure out your proper trade size.

IMPORTANT NOTE: For some advanced traders, it is beneficial to
risk more than 2 percent of their trading account. The amount these
traders risk must be carefully calculated depending on their proven
historical performance statistics. See Chapter 9 for the formulas to
determine if your payoff ratio and win ratio performance warrant a
higher risk than 2 percent.

TRADE SIZE FORMULA

In our example, we can risk $500 on a $25,000 trading account. The formula
for determining proper trade size for this risk amount is as follows:

Formula: [Risk amount − Commission]
         ÷ Difference between entry and exit = Trade size

Example: [$500 − $80] ÷ $1.50 = 280 shares

Details:
- Trading account size: $25,000
- 2 percent risk allowance: $500
- MSFT trade entry value: $60 per share
- MSFT initial stop: $58.50 per share
- Difference between entry and stop: $1.50
- Commission: $80 round trip
- Maximum trade size: 280 shares

Your trading system says to go long now at $60 per share. Your initial stop-loss exit is at $58.50, and the difference between your entry at $60 and your initial stop-loss exit at $58.50 is $1.50 per share. How many shares (trade size) can you buy when your risk is $1.50 per share and your 2 percent account risk is $500? The answer is: $500 − $80 (commissions) = $420. Then, $420 divided by $1.50 (difference between entry and stop amount) = 280 shares.

TRADE SIZE FORMULA USING LEVERAGE

Formula: [Risk amount − Commission]

÷ Difference between entry and stop = Trade size

Example: [$1,000 − $51.22] ÷ $1.26 = 753 shares

Details:
- Trading account size: $50,000
- Amount of margin: 150%
- Trading account size (using margin): $75,000
- 2 percent risk allowance (on $50,000): $1,000
- IBM trade entry value: $91.49 per share
- IBM initial stop: $90.23 per share
- Difference between entry and stop: $1.26
- Commission: $51.22
- Initial purchase of 753 shares at $91.49 = $68,891.97 IBM
- Actual dollar amount of margin at entry: $18,891.97 IBM
- Maximum trade size: 753 shares

The 2 percent risk formula takes into consideration the entry price, the initial stop-loss exit price, commission cost, and the dollar amount of the trading account. Therefore, it is possible to use leverage (margin) to produce the maximum trade size based on this rule.

For example, if we entered an IBM stock trade at $91.49 and our initial stop-loss exit is set at $90.23, then our maximum trade size would be 753 shares based on an account size of $50,000, a commission cost of $51.22 using 150 percent margin. Our actual dollar margin amount would be $18,891.97, but our risk on the trade, if stopped out, would be $1,000, or 2 percent of $50,000. Here, we are using margin while keeping the trade risk within 2 percent.

USING THE TRADE SIZE CALCULATOR

You can certainly do manual handwritten calculations for the formulas presented here, but I developed some simple software that makes it easier and faster to make these calculations during the trading day. It's called the *Trade Size Calculator*™ and a free 30-day trial of the software comes with the purchase of this book. Take a look at Figure 10.1 to see an illustration of how the calculator is used. Then you can refer to Appendix A for all the information on how to download your free trial of the software from the TradersCoach.com Web site.

TRADE SIZE CALCULATOR EXAMPLE

Take a look at Figure 10.1 to see an example of using the Trade Size Calculator software to determine your trade size. Here you will see that the specifics of the trade are as follows:

- Account size = $50,000
- Percent of capital at risk = 2 percent
- Trade entry price = $26.89
- Initial trade exit price = $25.45
- Risk amount per share = $1.54
- Commission = $10 round trip

On Figure 10.1 you can see that the risk amount is the distance between the trade entry price and the initial stop-loss exit price. That amount of risk comes to $1.54 per share and is indicated by an arrow pointing to the entry and arrow pointing to the initial stop-loss exit. After entering the specifics of the trade into the calculator, you see the following results:

- Maximum trade size = 642 shares
- Dollar risk = $998.68

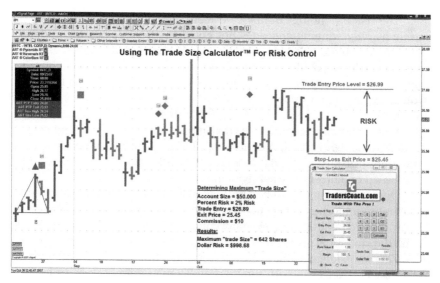

FIGURE 10.1   Illustration of the Trade Size Calculator Determining Proper Trade Size.
Source: eSignal.www.eSignal.com

You can manually determine the proper trade size using the formula in this chapter, but as you can see, it is quick and easy to use the calculator. Be sure to use your free 30-trial of the software, and go to Appendix A to see how to download your software from the TradersCoach. com Web site.

TRADE SIZE AND RISK PSYCHOLOGY

When someone makes a killing in the market on a relatively small or average trading account, this trader most likely was not implementing sound money management and had not developed a healthy risk psychology.

In cases such as this, the trader is more than likely exposed to obscene risk because of an abnormally large trade size, possibly using margin and leverage. In this case, the trader—or gambler—may have gotten lucky, which led to a profit windfall. If the trader continues trading in this way, the risk-of-ruin (ROR) probabilities suggest that it is just a matter of time before huge losses will dwarf the wins.

When someone tells me that he or she trades the exact same number of shares or contracts on every trade, I know that trader is not calculating the optimal trade size. Otherwise, the trade size would change from time to time to reflect changing market dynamics.

The risk psychology of novice traders tends to focus on the trade outcome as only winning and does not consider the risk. Master traders instead focus on the risk first and take a trade based on a *probable* favorable outcome. The psychology behind trade size begins when you believe and acknowledge that each trade's outcome is unknown. Believing this makes you ask yourself, how much can I afford to lose and not fall prey to the risk of ruin?

When traders ask themselves this question, they will either adjust their trade size or tighten their stop-loss exit before entering the trade. In most situations, the best method is to adjust the trade size and set your stop-loss exit based on current market dynamics.

During account drawdown periods, risk control and trade size become even more important. Since master traders test their trading systems, they know the probabilities of how many consecutive losses they may incur, and what the statistical probabilities are regarding drawdown and their system.

This knowledge enables them to resist the temptation to either give up or to try and get even with the market. They are more likely to maintain an even keel and reap the benefits on future well-managed trades. This risk psychology and confidence takes time and experience to develop.

Record Keeping and Profit/Loss Analysis

CHAPTER 11

Tracking Profit and Loss Results and More Formulas for Success

T here are many reasons you'll benefit from setting up a system to track your profit and loss results. Initially, discipline is the primary reason. The discipline you develop in your accounting of profit and loss results, and your other vital statistics, will transfer over into your day-to-day success.

As you finely tune your trading machine by evaluating results, you'll find that it's easier to follow your trading system rules, you will become more disciplined overall, and there will be less doubt and more confidence in your trading system. It's a perpetual process, and there are an infinite number of intangible benefits.

BENEFITS FROM MAINTAINING A CONSISTENT RECORD KEEPING SYSTEM

There are at least ten benefits to maintaining good record keeping:

1. It adds discipline to your overall approach.
2. Confidence and awareness are increased in your trading system.
3. You can confront and correct losing behavior more quickly so you can take action to prevent risk of ruin, plus you will reduce any tendency for denial or avoidance of reality.

4. You can recognize *true* winning behavior, as opposed to *perceived* winning behavior, more quickly so you can take action and duplicate your winning behaviors and techniques going forward.

5. The possibility of denial in trading psychology is reduced, and the overall psychology is improved.

6. Good record keeping provides a constant barometer of current vital statistics, such as your win ratio and payoff ratio, so you can determine the percent of risk you can allow on each trade to avoid the risk of ruin.

7. Thorough records for tax preparation are at your fingertips.

8. It establishes professionalism and commitment.

9. You can recognize trading errors and implement procedures to reduce the chance of repeating them in the future.

10. You can increase your control (both perceived and real) over your trading destiny—it is far better psychologically to be in the driver's seat and have the feeling of control over your future.

AN APPLE A DAY (OR ANALYSIS EVERY DAY) KEEPS THE TRADING DOCTOR AWAY

It probably seems obvious that there are benefits to record keeping of some type or another. Let's define the *regularity* of the record keeping that we're suggesting, so that you do not misunderstand the concepts discussed.

To pull your trading records and a calculator together once a month (or even once a week) to determine how your return on investment (ROI) is doing is *not* what I want you to do. The plan here is to take inventory *every* single active trading day from this day forward. Then the goal is to have the discipline to consistently conduct your analysis *every* day going forward so that you can keep the doctor away. This requires that you make the commitment right here and right now to develop your self-awareness.

The value of self awareness by means of your record keeping is that you cannot live in a comfortable state of *denial* when you are losing money in your trading. It is easy to avoid unpleasant truths when you do not run the numbers every day. You may suspect that one trade or another may have been handled incorrectly, but until you do the analysis it is all too easy to ignore your mistakes. Awareness of your mistakes and what caused them is what will make you a more profitable trader.

Another issue to clarify is that analysis is *not* just determining if you were profitable or not profitable, end of story. It goes deeper than that and requires a little bit of math to evaluate some vital statistics that you should know every day. We'll get into the specifics of these vitals in just a minute.

MAKE THE COMMITMENT

Have you mentally and physically made the commitment to focus your resources on tracking profit and loss and vital statistics? If the answer is no, then we need to find out why there is resistance to this concept.

Here are a few questions:

Q1. Is it too much work?

Q2. Does it seem overwhelming?

Q3. Have you tracked results before and it didn't seem to help?

Q4. Are you *not* inclined to be analytical in nature, are you not motivated by the details, are you more motivated by the big picture, the big idea, and the big breakthrough?

Q5. Psychologically, is it uncomfortable to see that you are *losing*—is it more comfortable to postpone the news, maybe in the hope that it will correct itself?

Q6. Psychologically, is it uncomfortable to see that you are *winning*—is it more comfortable to not know for sure? Is there pressure to continue winning—are you only as good as your last winning streak?

Q7. Do you feel that record keeping is not the answer to greater profits—that the answer is in focusing your resources to find a better trading system?

These questions can uncover important clues in determining how you will move forward in your record keeping approach. Consider the following answers and comments to the previous questions:

A1. If you feel that record keeping is too much work, do you consider yourself a lazy person? If you are traditionally lazy, then trading may not be the right fit for you, since it will require a certain amount of effort in order to be successful. If you are traditionally *not* lazy, then you have to ask yourself why it feels like too much work.

A2. If you feel that record keeping is overwhelming, then you will need to break it down into small steps so that you can successful accomplish each step one at a time. Do not attempt to tackle the entire job at once; use baby steps.

A3. If you have tracked results before and it didn't seem to help your profit performance, then possibly the record keeping system wasn't geared toward identifying the right statistics. Give the program in this book a chance, and see if the suggestions here might enable you to get insight into how you can improve your profitability.

A4. If you are not typically an analytical person, meaning you are more of a right-brain thinker, then maybe there is someone you can delegate your record keeping to. It is common for traders to have a partner, wife, husband, or employee who does their accounting. Brainstorm and determine who might be the right person for the job. This way, you don't get paralyzed by having to do something you hate to do, or are not good at doing.

A5. If you are psychologically uncomfortable with facing information that tells you about losing trades, then you most likely have not fully developed your trading psychology and the trader's mindset. This is an area you will want to focus on going forward. In the meantime, it is crucial that you power through and, like Nike says, "Just do it!" Just force yourself to do the numbers. This in itself may enable you to improve your psychology and profitability.

A6. If you are psychologically uncomfortable with facing information that you have winning trades, you have not fully developed your trading psychology and the trader's mindset. Just as with A5, this is an area you will want to focus on going forward. In the meantime, it is crucial that you power through and just do it!

A7. If you believe that record keeping is not going to be helpful in generating greater profits and that your time would be better spent on finding a better trading system, then you need to read Chapter 3. Your current belief system indicates that you have not fully developed your trading psychology and the trader's mindset. Again, as with items A5 and A6, it is probably best for you to bite the bullet, stick with your current system for now, and just do it! Just start record keeping and give it an opportunity to prove that it has merit.

I hope this list of questions and answers about possible hesitations to incorporating a solid record keeping system will spark some thought in your mind as to how to proceed. Ultimately, you will be better off with a regular record keeping system. I urge you to confront whatever resistance you may have so that you can start benefiting from this plan now.

RECORD KEEPING IS THE RX FOR SUCCESS

Record keeping is the prescription for success. This is where you will be the doctor that will collect vital statistics, analyze those statistics and determine the prognosis, and then prescribe the necessary medicine for getting healthy.

DETERMINE YOUR CURRENT TRADING VITAL STATISTICS

Have you ever noticed that when you go to the doctor or hospital, the nurses are constantly taking your "vitals"? With good reason, because that is the only way they can determine what will be the best prescription and diagnosis for better health. Here are the vital statistics you will need to track going forward:

- Win ratio
- Payoff ratio
- Commission ratio
- Largest winning trade
- Largest losing trade
- Average winning trade
- Average losing trade
- Largest number of consecutive losses
- Average number of consecutive losses
- Largest trading account percent of drawdown
- Average trading account percent of drawdown

These statistics will give you the historical data to adjust your money management system and occasionally adjust your trading system to adapt to ever-fluctuating market conditions. In the next chapter, you will learn how to track these statistics using The Trader's Assistant record keeping system.

MEDICAL VITAL STATISTICS HELP WITH DIAGNOSIS

Doctors and nurses are in the business of collecting vital statistics every day, and there is much to be learned from this. For them, it is second nature, just as it should be for traders.

As an analogy we can look at our trading vitals in the same way that a doctor looks at our medical vitals. As an illustration, let's list some vital statistics that are commonly used in medicine:

1. Blood pressure
2. Weight and height
3. Temperature
4. Medical history
5. Oxygen level in the blood
6. Cholesterol
7. Current symptoms
8. Family medical history
9. Age
10. Surgical history

Many of these medical vitals are similar to our trading vitals. For example, your trading history can help predict your future trading patterns. Your trading temperature is a quick barometer to let you know if your current trading temperature is normal—are you 98.6?

Your current trading symptoms will help you determine what to prescribe. If your payoff ratio is high but your percent of wins to losses is low, you know that you want to prescribe a plan to increase your wins to losses. This is valuable analysis, and it will be instrumental in boosting your profits.

FORMULAS FOR SUCCESS

The three important vital statistic ratios you will need to calculate are:

1. Win ratio
2. Payoff ratio
3. Commission ratio

These ratios tell you your current standing on a variety of levels and will give you guidance on how to move forward. Use the following formulas to calculate your vital statistics.

WIN RATIO FORMULA

This is the percent of winning trades to losing trades. The more winning trades you have, the better, although in trading you will never have 100 percent winning trades. This ratio may fluctuate day to day, and it is important for you to constantly observe the ratio to determine if there has been a market cycle change or to determine if you are experiencing a normal drawdown.

When your win ratio is low, there is the possibility of *pilot error*, or basically, human error. Determine what might be causing the human error issue—fatigue, poor psychology, and so on—so that you can address the situation and make the necessary adjustments.

Formula:
Win ratio = Number of winning trades ÷ Total number of trades

To get a percentage, multiply the ratio by 100.
Example:
60% = 60 ÷ 100

PAYOFF RATIO FORMULA

This is the ratio that tells you how many dollars you earn for every dollar you lose. The higher your payoff ratio, the better. If you are consistently earning $3 for every $1 you lose (3 to 1), you can be proud of yourself. If you are earning $1 for every $1 you lose, you are breaking even and you will need to determine how to improve this ratio. Very often, a sound money management system will enable you to improve this ratio.

Formula:
Payoff ratio = Average winning trade ÷ Average losing trade
Example:
3 = $300 ÷ $100

COMMISSION RATIO FORMULA

This is the percent of your profits that go toward paying commission to your broker. When you are overtrading, the percentage of your profits that goes toward paying commission will go up. This figure can be a barometer to tell you when you are overtrading. For example if you have a commission ratio of 90% you are giving 90 percent of your profits to the broker. This means you want to make fewer trades while still making the same profit—that way you get to keep more of your winnings. Another cause for high commission ratios is poor payoff ratios. For example if 60 percent of your trades are winners you will have a more favorable commission ratio than if 25 percent of your trades are winners.

Formula:
Commission ratio = Total commission paid ÷ Total Gross profit

To get a percentage, multiply the ratio by 100.

Example:
20% = $200 ÷ $1000

Note: This formula is not applicable if your payoff ratio is less than 1 to 1. If you are not generating a profit you can not calculate your commission ratio.

CONSISTENT RETURN ON INVESTMENT

This chapter has been devoted to the importance of tracking your profit and loss. These statistics will be valuable in determining what your ROI is, and that is what this business, and every business, is all about. When trading you are making an investment of your time and money in order to obtain a consistent monetary return. The key is to ensure that your return is just that—consistent. By implementing a money management plan, you will increase your chances of maintaining a consistent profit margin in your trading.

CHAPTER 12

Using Trade Posting Cards and Ledgers

T his chapter shows you how to use the Trader's Assistant to keep your trading records by using trade posting cards and ledgers. The terrific thing about the instructions in this chapter is that you will see actual results from a trading student of mine that paper traded for one full year and was generous enough to let me share with you his performance results. The illustrations of these posting cards and trade ledgers in use will give you an immediate understanding of how tracking your performance will benefit your bottom line.

NOW YOU'RE A TRADING ACCOUNTANT

If you don't want to be a trading accountant, you need to get yourself a bookkeeper or an assistant to keep up to date with your records. What we are providing you with in this book is a complete system that gives you all the forms, cards, and ledgers to track the vital information you will need. Now it will be your job to implement that system.

Many traders employ the assistance of a partner, wife, husband, accountant, or bookkeeper to stay on top of the numbers. If that works best for you, it is certainly better than doing something you dislike or may not be good at. Of course, the analysis part of this equation cannot be delegated; you must do your own analysis.

WHAT IS INCLUDED IN THE TRADER'S ASSISTANT RECORD KEEPING SYSTEM

The Trader's Assistant is a system that will help you track your trades from a macro level to a micro level. What this means is that you will be able to take a look at your performance from the macro level on the annual trade ledger all the way down to the micro level on each individual trade-posting card.

Here are the nine different forms that are included in *The Trader's Assistant* system you will find in Appendix B:

1. Daily worksheet
2. Daily trade ledger
3. Weekly trade ledger
4. Monthly trade ledger
5. Annual trade ledger
6. Stock trade posting card
7. Option trade posting card
8. Future trade posting card
9. Trading Scorecard

By completing these forms daily, weekly, monthly, and annually, you will be capturing the data you need from both a profit/loss standpoint and also from a trading psychology standpoint. This unique personal data, over time, holds the key to improving your performance.

TRACKING YOUR PSYCHOLOGY

Not only will you be tracking the numbers with the tools we will give you, but also you will be tracking your psychology. Seeing how your thoughts and feelings impact the outcome of each transaction is valuable in giving you a window into your own psyche.

With this said, remember to *always* write down your emotional reasons for taking a trade, in addition to the fundamental and technical reasons. You must note these down as they happen, since, in hindsight, you will never get an accurate reading on what you really were thinking or feeling at the time.

USE *THE TRADER'S ASSISTANT* RECORD KEEPING SYSTEM

Back in 1995 when trading in New York City, my own trading needs prompted me to develop a record keeping system for myself, since there was none on the market. This system was later named *The Trader's Assistant* and is now available to you for your own record keeping.

Refer to Appendix B at the back of this book, where you will find blank forms that you can photocopy and implement into your own money management program. I developed this system for my own use and benefit from it every day. My hope is that it will elevate your money management to a new level, where you will increase your profits dramatically.

Remember, this record system works for any market and any time frame. So if you are an investor, position trader, or day trader, the system will help you track your results.

THIS IS YOUR HAND-WRITTEN SCORECARD

The Trader's Assistant system you'll be using from this book (you can find the blank forms in Appendix B) will be hand-written, and that is intentional on my part. I want you to hand-write your statistics, so that you will be more connected to your results and the process. Your brain functions on many levels, and the sensory system is a valuable tool in gaining access to your inner psyche.

Whenever possible while learning and growing, try to use all five senses: sight, sound, touch, taste, and smell. Taste and smell might be metaphorical senses in this case, as in "Get a taste of success" and "This smells like disaster." But, I want you to understand that the more you immerse yourself into the process, the more productive the outcome will be. You want to hear, see, write, and talk about the information, really integrate it. Find a trading partner, coach, or buddy with whom you can further brainstorm and gain access to this sensory development idea.

So, as much as I do love computers, my process of record keeping on the intake level is always hand-written. Keep in mind, there are times when your electrical power can fail (brown-outs and black-outs), or when your computer will crash, and it is these times when you will be grateful for your hand-written trade posting cards, so that you will know what the latest entries and exits were on all of your positions. This in itself can be a life saver.

Some of my students ultimately pour their statistics into an Excel spreadsheet and do some additional number crunching, but they report back to me that they appreciate the hand-written input phase. One student says that when he inputs the numbers into his Excel spreadsheet, it acts as an *audit*, since there are times when inconsistencies occur and, as it turns out, corrections need to be made.

A YEAR IN THE LIFE OF A TRADING STUDENT

In this chapter are illustrations of *The Trader's Assistant* trade posting cards and ledgers filled out and in actual use. These are examples from a real live first-year trading student of mine that has paper traded the *Applied Reality Trading (ART)* software for one full year. This student was generous enough to share these records with me, and now with you, so that we could see an entire year of actual simulated trading, including the ups and downs and the learning process.

Keep in mind that this student day trades the Nasdaq 100 and the futures market, but *The Trader's Assistant* record keeping system works on any market and any time frame. So if you are not a day trader and you don't trade these markets, this record keeping system will work equally well for you. Just apply the same principles to your own market and time frame.

This student has now proceeded to live trading with real money, but the practice of paper trading for one full year has provided him with a foundation of historical data to confidently follow through with his money management system. From this data he is able to determine all the vital statistics needed to be successful.

As most of my students know, I am a big fan of paper trading, because I see how well it works. A number of trading professionals discount the paper-trading process as not valuable because they believe you won't feel the same emotions as you do with real money. But, I have to disagree, because if you are treating the paper trading as your test before you go live in the market, you will feel similar emotions. You want to pass the test, and you want to go live, so any setback will generate similar feelings to the real thing.

Now, you don't necessarily need to paper trade for an entire year, but you do want to paper trade until you prove your profitability for a consistent period of time and prove that the system you are using is compatible with your personality. If for some reason you are absolutely against paper trading, use a *mini account* instead. This means you should trade only a small portion of your actual trading capital first to get your feet wet.

　　In the following sections of this chapter, we will review the ledgers and cards working from the macro level (the annual trade ledger) down to the micro level (each individual trade posting card).

ANNUAL TRADE LEDGER EXAMPLE

This is the ultimate scorecard that in a glance tells you the entire story of your year. In my student's example, he is paper trading with an account size of $25,000.

Annual Trade Ledger for 2007, 50.7 Percent Gain

The information we gain from the annual trade ledger (see Figure 12.1) and the account size of $25,000, we can determine these twelve vital statistics for the year:

1. Win ratio: 39% wins
2. Payoff ratio: $1.96 win to $1.00 loss
3. Commission ratio: 25% of gross profits go to commission
4. Largest winning trade: $2,814.14
5. Largest losing trade: ($621.72)
6. Average winning trade: $559.50
7. Average losing trade: ($285.59)
8. Largest number of consecutive losses: 7
9. Average number of consecutive losses: 4
10. Largest trading account % drawdown: 12%
11. Average trading account % drawdown: 6%
12. Annualized profit/loss on trading account: 50.7% profit

　　The annual ledger gives you a lot of valuable information to help you focus on trading system issues, as well as money management issues. Let's do a quick analysis of what we have learned from this annual trade ledger:

- November was the most profitable month.
- June had a dramatic drawdown.
- Annual net profitable return on investment was 50.7 percent.
- Commissions eat up 25 percent of gross profits.
- Payoff ratio is $1.96 wins to each $1.00 loss.

TradersCoach.com
Tc "The Trader's Assistant"—A Trade Posting and Record Keeping System

YEAR OF LEDGER
2007

ANNUAL TRADE LEDGER

MONTH	# TRADES	# WINNING	# LOSING	GROSS $ P/L	COMMISSION $	NET $ P/L	RUNNING NET $ P/L
JANUARY	46	21	25	4295.00	(600.92)	3694.08	3694.08
FEBRUARY	28	9	19	(320.00)	(459.74)	(779.74)	2914.34
MARCH	13	5	8	(615.00)	(202.72)	(817.72)	2096.62
APRIL	32	14	18	3345.00	(524.90)	2820.10	4916.72
MAY	28	9	19	1062.51	(325.80)	736.71	5653.43
JUNE	29	7	22	(2600.00)	(325.80)	(2925.80)	2727.62
JULY	23	8	15	(5.00)	(394.58)	(399.58)	2328.04
AUGUST	33	14	19	2837.50	(275.12)	2562.38	4890.42
SEPTEMBER	16	5	11	650.00	(162.90)	487.10	5377.52
OCTOBER	21	9	12	2237.50	(191.86)	2045.64	7423.16
NOVEMBER	33	13	20	3937.50	(224.44)	3713.06	11'136.22
DECEMBER	21	9	12	850.00	(285.98)	564.02	11'700.24
TOTALS:	323	123	200	15'675.00	(3974.76)	11'700.24	

LARGEST WINNING TRADE OF THE YEAR:	$ 2814.14	LARGEST WINNING TRADE POSTING CARD #:	297-07	AVERAGE WINNING TRADE OF THE YEAR:	$ 559.50
LARGEST LOSING TRADE OF THE YEAR:	$ (621.72)	LARGEST LOSING TRADE POSTING CARD #:	315-07	AVERAGE LOSING TRADE OF THE YEAR:	$ (285.59)

NOTES:

My first year of trading ended well

I am UP 51%

My annual pay-off ratio is: $1.96 to $1.00

My annual win ratio is: 39%

111802

FIGURE 12.1 Student Annual Trade Ledger On $25,000 Paper Trading Account for 2007, 50.7 Percent Gain.

- Win ratio is currently 39 percent wins, which could be improved. Review entry and exit strategy, look for patterns on winning trades that could be replicated more consistently.
- Drawdown can last for 7 consecutive trades, and can deplete the account by 12 percent. Adapt and strengthen trading psychology to know that this is possible.

These are just a few observations that can be helpful in evaluating this year's performance. There is always room for improvement, but it is also important to acknowledge the positive. In this example, the annual return is 50.7 percent, which is terrific for a first-year student. The greatest area for improvement would be increasing the number of wins, and that is very achievable with some observation and analysis.

Your results may be very different than these examples, and you will want to creatively analyze your results to see where your strengths are and where you have room for improvement.

Remember, any improvement is good improvement. For example, if you are paper trading and losing $1,000 every month and you reduce that loss to $500 a month, you have done a great job. Then it is a matter of continuing the work to beat the market and consistently get in the black and generate profits.

Work on all cylinders, money management, trading system, trading psychology, and so on. When you have a balance of skills in all of these areas your profits will increase. Usually it is the weakest link that determines the overall strength of the chain. So, it is best to work on your weakest link, and keep strengthening the chain links—each and every one.

BEAT THE MARKET

"Beat the market" seems to be a popular phrase these days; however, your goal should be to do more than beat the market; you want to completely pummel the market and then some. And you can do so by honing and fine tuning both your money management system and your trading system.

They both work hand in hand, and you will gain important knowledge from your record keeping that can assist you in adjusting your entry and exit strategies just by observing the characteristics of your winning and losing trades. Again, replicate the winning scenarios and avoid the losing scenarios.

Looking at my first-year trading student's annual paper-trading ledger, he more than beat the market. The average annual yield for the market is around 10 percent, and he certainly beat the market with an annual yield of over 50 percent. Of course he is paper trading, and it is not exactly the same as live trades. But, it's been my experience that when my students do this much paper trading prior to entering the market, they have already honed their approach, and their live market results are very similar to their paper trading.

The bottom line is that you want to beat the market and then some, so go for it and make it happen. Use the power of intention and generate profits.

MONTHLY TRADE LEDGER EXAMPLES

As we focus on the profit/loss results of my student, we are going to look at both a profitable month and an unprofitable month. This can show how the vital statistics can dramatically vary from month to month. It is important that your trading psychology is developed so that one bad trade, one bad day, one bad week, or one bad month does not send you into a tailspin or into paralysis.

Learn from the good trades and from the bad trades, and use your record keeping to do that. Observation is the tool that scientists and doctors use to develop giant discoveries and breakthroughs in their work. You are not different, you may be reviewing your records and have one of those aha! or eureka! moments that may change the future of your trading. Embrace these moments and cherish them. By doing so, you are likely to have more of them to come.

Monthly Trade Ledger for January 2007, 15 Percent Gain

Let's start by reviewing the monthly trading ledger for January (see Figure 12.2). This was one of the most profitable months of the year, and ideally, we would like to replicate these results as often as possible. Here are the eight vital statistics for the month of January:

1. Win ratio: 46 percent
2. Payoff ratio: $1.91 win to $1.00 loss
3. Commission ratio: 14 percent of gross profits go to commission
4. Largest winning trade: $2,009.14
5. Largest losing trade: ($475.86)
6. Average winning trade: $468.94

TradersCoach.com
"The Trader's Assistant"—A Trade Posting and Record Keeping System

MONTHLY TRADE LEDGER

WEEK	# TRADES	# WINNING	# LOSING	GROSS $ P/L	COMMISSION $	NET $ P/L	RUNNING NET $ P/L
1	8	5	3	3435.00	(83.26)	3351.74	3351.74
1-01							
2	15	6	9	85.00	(199.10)	(114.10)	(3237.64)
1-08							
3	11	7	4	1225.00	(148.42)	1076.58	4314.22
1-15							
4	12	3	9	(450.00)	(170.14)	(620.14)	3694.08
1-22							
5	0	0	0				
1-29							
TOTALS:	46	21	25	4295.00	(600.92)	3694.08	

LARGEST WINNING TRADE OF THE MONTH:	$ 2009.14	LARGEST WINNING TRADE POSTING CARD #:	002-07	AVERAGE WINNING TRADE OF THE MONTH:	$ 468.94
LARGEST LOSING TRADE OF THE MONTH:	$ (475.86)	LARGEST LOSING TRADE POSTING CARD #:	043-07	AVERAGE LOSING TRADE OF THE MONTH:	$ (246.14)

NOTES:

15% gain for the month

Payoff ratio: $1.91 to $1.00

Win ratio: 46%

FIGURE 12.2 Student Monthly Trade Ledger for January 2007, 15 Percent Gain.

7. Average losing trade: ($246.14)

8. This month's profit/loss on trading account: 15 percent profit

What we learn from a significantly profitable month is the areas of strength we can work on duplicating. Here's a quick analysis of what we can learn from this monthly trade ledger:

- Win ratio is 46 percent for this month, much higher than the annual ratio of 39 percent. This confirms that the direction we want to continue in is to increase the win ratio.
- Payoff ratio is $1.91, right on target for the annual average.
- Commission ratio is 14 percent for this month. That is much lower than the annual commission ratio of 25 percent.
- The month of January had one of the largest winning trades of the year, with a profit of $2,009. We will take a look at the trade posting card for this trade later in this chapter to identify what characteristics of this trade we want to duplicate.
- No big news with regard to the average win and average loss—they are on target with the annual average.
- Big news on the profit of 15 percent on the trading account for this month

The observations for the month of January will be useful and will lead us to look further at the winning trade of $2,009.

Monthly Trade Ledger for June 2007, 12 Percent Loss

Now let's look at the most challenging month of this year, June (see Figure 12.3), where there was a loss of $2925.80. Here are the eight vital statistics for the month of June:

1. Win ratio: 24 percent

2. Payoff ratio: $1.80

3. Commission ratio: n/a

4. Largest winning trade: $1,335.52

5. Largest losing trade: ($460.83)

6. Average winning trade: $560.80

7. Average losing trade: ($311.43)

8. This month's profit/loss on trading account: 12 percent loss.

TradersCoach.com
"The Trader's Assistant"—A Trade Posting and Record Keeping System

MONTH OF LEDGER
JUNE 07

MONTHLY TRADE LEDGER

WEEK	# TRADES	# WINNING	# LOSING	GROSS $ P/L	COMMISSION $	NET $ P/L	RUNNING NET $ P/L
1 6-1	1 4	0 0	1 4	(375.00) (900.00)	(10.86) (54.30)	(385.86) (954.30)	(1340.16)
6-4							
2 6-11	6	2	4	637.50	(68.78)	568.72	(771.44)
3 6-18	4	1	3	(937.50)	(54.30)	(991.80)	(1763.24)
4 6-25	14	4	10	(1025.00)	(137.56)	(1162.56)	(2925.80)
5							
TOTALS:	29	7	22	(2600.00)	(325.80)	(2925.80)	

LARGEST WINNING TRADE OF THE MONTH:	$ 1,335.52	LARGEST WINNING TRADE POSTING CARD #:	171-07	AVERAGE WINNING TRADE OF THE MONTH:	$ 560.80
LARGEST LOSING TRADE OF THE MONTH:	$ (460.83)	LARGEST LOSING TRADE POSTING CARD #:	176-07	AVERAGE LOSING TRADE OF THE MONTH:	$ (311.43)

NOTES:

Loss for the month: (12%)

!! I need to call Ben!

Payoff ratio: $1.80 to $1.00

Win ratio: 24%

111802   Copyright © 2002 by **TradersCoach.com, Inc.**

FIGURE 12.3 Student Monthly Trade Ledger for June 2007, 12 Percent Loss.

We can also learn from the most unprofitable month by looking at weaknesses that can be worked on and improved. Here's a quick analysis of the month of June:

- Win ratio is in dangerous territory: 24 percent wins to 76 percent losses make it virtually impossible to come out ahead. This period certainly would be considered a drawdown period, and we can use the history to anticipate future drawdown activity.
- Payoff ratio is $1.80. This would be an adequate ratio if the win ratio were higher.
- Average win and loss figures are too close to each other in value, again not a disaster if the win ratio had been higher.
- Loss on the trading account is 12 percent for this month, significant and important to analyze to determine if there were any trading errors that could be identified and avoided in the future.

It is important to compare your strong trading periods with your weak trading periods to identify valuable insights and observations.

WEEKLY TRADE LEDGER EXAMPLES

We're closing in on the micro level of the analysis to the point where we get to look at actual emotions and trading psychology and how that also plays into the numbers in a very real way. As before we'll look at two examples of my student's trade ledgers; one is a profitable week and one is a losing week.

Weekly Trade Ledger for January 22, 2007, 2 Percent Loss

The first week is from January 22, and shows a net loss of $620.14 (see Figure 12.4). Let's take a look at this week's vital statistics:

1. Win ratio: 25 percent
2. Payoff ratio: 77 cents win for every $1 lost
3. Commission ratio: N/A
4. Largest winning trade: $1,761.90
5. Largest losing trade: ($475.86)
6. Average winning trade: $701
7. Average losing trade: $303
8. This week's profit/loss on trading account: 2 percent loss for the week

TradersCoach.com

"The Trader's Assistant"—A Trade Posting and Record Keeping System

WEEK # OF THIS LEDGER (CIRCLE ONE)
1   2   3   (4)   5
MONDAY'S DATE FOR THIS WEEK
JAN 22, 07

WEEKLY TRADE LEDGER

DAY	# TRADES	# WINNING	# LOSING	GROSS $ P/L	COMMISSION $	NET $ P/L	RUNNING NET $ P/L
MONDAY 1-22	1	1	0	45.00	(10.86)	34.14	34.14
TUESDAY 1-23	3	0	3	(855.00)	(47.06)	(902.06)	(867.92)
WEDNESDAY 1-24	1	1	0	325.00	(18.10)	306.90	(561.02)
THURSDAY 1-25	3	1	2	1055.00	(50.68)	1004.32	443.30
FRIDAY 1-26	4	0	4	(1020.00)	(43.44)	(1063.44)	(620.14)
SATURDAY							
SUNDAY							
TOTALS:	12	3	9	(450.00)	(170.14)	(620.14)	

LARGEST WINNING TRADE OF THE WEEK:	$ 1761.90	LARGEST WINNING TRADE POSTING CARD #:	042-07	AVERAGE WINNING TRADE OF THE WEEK:	$ 701.00
LARGEST LOSING TRADE OF THE WEEK:	$ (475.86)	LARGEST LOSING TRADE POSTING CARD #:	043-07	AVERAGE LOSING TRADE OF THE WEEK:	$ (303.00)

NOTES:

Mixed week: I only had 3 wins

Frustration was the last day with 4 losses in a row.

Win ratio: 25%

Payoff ratio: 0.77

111802   Copyright © 2002 by TradersCoach.com, Inc.

FIGURE 12.4 Student Weekly Trade Ledger for January 22, 2007, 2 Percent Loss.

This weekly ledger is interesting in that it occurs at the end of a very profitable month of the year we are using as an example, which is the month of January. Here are some observations on the trading psychology and the performance that unfolded during this week:

- At the bottom of this ledger in the notes section, my student commented: "Mixed week: I only had 3 wins; frustration was on the last day with four losses in a row" . . .
- What is interesting about capturing this insight into his feelings is that this was a fabulously successful month, and the week in this example posted a loss of only $620, which, when looked at in perspective, is relatively small.
- Considering that January was the first month of trading and success seemed to come quickly, the question is, was there some discomfort with the success coming right away?
- Yes, the win ratio and payoff ratio are dismal for this week, but for an isolated week it is a manageable setback.
- Looking at the following two months, February and March, there is a small loss posted, but then the month of April is back on track.
- These are normal cycles of trading, and to become accustomed to ups and downs creates an advantage for you and your trading psychology.

Weekly Trade Ledger for July 23, 2007, 9 Percent Gain

The next weekly ledger (see Figure 12.5) we are going to look at follows a significant drawdown period that took place in June and July. Let's look at the eight vital statistics for the week of July 23, 2007:

1. Win ratio: 80 percent
2. Payoff ratio: $2.21
3. Commission ratio: 1%
4. Largest winning trade: $992.76
5. Largest losing trade: ($291.12)
6. Average winning trade: $643.67
7. Average losing trade: ($291.12)
8. This week's profit/loss on trading account: 9 percent profit

This was a terrific week—*the most profitable week of the year*. Again, it follows a severe drawdown period that was psychologically difficult. Having the continuous cycle and rhythm of trades over time does make

TradersCoach.com

TC "The Trader's Assistant"—A Trade Posting and Record Keeping System

WEEK # OF THIS LEDGER (CIRCLE ONE)

1 2 3 (4) 5

MONDAY'S DATE FOR THIS WEEK

JULY 23, 07

WEEKLY TRADE LEDGER

DAY	# TRADES	# WINNING	# LOSING	GROSS $ P/L	COMMISSION $	NET $ P/L	RUNNING NET $ P/L
MONDAY 7-23	NO TRADES						
TUESDAY 7-24	1	1	0	875.00	(7.24)	867.76	867.76
WEDNESDAY 7-25	1	1	0	600.00	(7.24)	592.76	1460.52
THURSDAY 7-26	2	1	1	(162.50)	(7.24)	(169.74)	1290.78
FRIDAY 7-27	1	1	0	1000.00	(7.24)	992.76	2283.54
SATURDAY							
SUNDAY							
TOTALS:	5	4	1	2312.50	(28.96)	2283.54	

LARGEST WINNING TRADE OF THE WEEK:	$ 992.76	LARGEST WINNING TRADE POSTING CARD #:	198-07	AVERAGE WINNING TRADE OF THE WEEK:	$ 643.67
LARGEST LOSING TRADE OF THE WEEK:	$ (291.12)	LARGEST LOSING TRADE POSTING CARD #:	196-07	AVERAGE LOSING TRADE OF THE WEEK:	$ (291.12)

NOTES:

It was a better week. I was able to record some good gains. Dow dropped a huge amount (<586.26 pts). Nasdaq lost 136.25 pts. -5.05%. The Emini S&P 500 that I traded dropped 85.75 pts (-5.55%). All this happened a week after the market posted record highs (Dow: 14000.41 close, 14021.95 high). Indeed, it was a very big correction. I am sure I could have done better. For instance on 7-26-07, if I would have chosen the 3' time frame, I would have made a nice profit instead of a small loss. BUT HAVE TO CHOOSE THE RIGHT TIME FRAME THAT IS THE QUESTION.

Win ratio: 80%
Payoff ratio: 2.2
Commission ratio: 1%

FIGURE 12.5 Student Weekly Trade Ledger for July 23, 2007, 9 Percent Gain.

attaining The Trader's Mindset easier. The cycles become second nature. Of course, with experience the management of the cycles gets more efficient. Let's look over the numbers:

- Exceptional win ratio of 80 percent; this is the direction we want to continue in. The annual win ratio is 39 percent wins, so this week my student doubled the number of wins, and it certainly boosted the bottom line.
- Commission ratio was outstanding, with only 1 percent of the profit going to pay the broker. This is compared to the annual ratio of 25 percent being paid in commissions. Certainly, there are added benefits to raising your win ratio, and that is reduced commission expenses.
- The notes at the bottom of my student's ledger read: "It was a better week. I was able to record some good gain. Dow dropped a huge amount, down 586 points. Nasdaq lost 136 points, down 5 percent. The Eminis S&P 500 that I traded dropped 85 points, down 5.5 percent. All of this happened a week after the market posted record highs (DOW 14,000). Indeed it was a very big correction this week. I am sure I could have done better. For instance on 7/26/07 if I would have chosen the 3-minute time frame, I could have made a very nice profit instead of a small loss. But, how to choose the time frame, that is the question!"
- There is a lot to be learned from reviewing the notes you'll be putting on your ledgers. For example, here this trader recognizes that selecting the right time frame has a great impact on profitability. Therefore, on future trades he'll be more aware of his techniques and how to implement them.

DAILY TRADE LEDGER EXAMPLE

The daily ledger is really just a compilation of all of your individual trade posting cards for the day. The daily ledger lists all the filled orders. Your most meaningful notes will be found on each individual posting card (see Figure 12.6).

DAILY WORKSHEET EXAMPLE

This form is used in conjunction with the daily ledger so that you can list all your placed orders. Only your filled orders will go onto a trade posting card or onto your final daily trade ledger (see Figure 12.7).

TradersCoach.com
"The Trader's Assistant"—A Trade Posting and Record Keeping System

TODAY'S DATE
SEPTEMBER 6, 07

DAILY TRADE LEDGER — Filled Orders

Open Position Trades Carried Forward

POSITION TRADE NUMBER	POSTING CARD NUMBER	SYMBOL	POSITION	SHARES	BOUGHT $	SOLD $	GROSS $ P/L	COMM $	NET $ P/L	RUNNING NET $ P/L
1										
2										
3										
4										
5										
POSITION TRADE TOTALS ———————➤										

New Trades Filled Today

TODAY'S TRADE NUMBER	POSTING CARD NUMBER	SYMBOL	POSITION	SHARES	BOUGHT $	SOLD $	GROSS $ P/L	COMM $	NET $ P/L	RUNNING NET $ P/L
1	233-07	ESU7	SHORT	2	1474.50	1471.00	(350.00)	(7.24)	(357.24)	(357.24)
2	234-07	ESU7	SHORT	4	1479.50	1482.50	600.00	(14.48)	585.52	228.28
3										
4										
5										
6										
7										
8										
9										
10										
DAY TRADE TOTALS ———————————➤							250.00	(21.72)	228.28	
GRAND TOTALS ———————————————➤										

LARGEST WINNING TRADE OF THE DAY:	$ 585.52	LARGEST WINNING TRADE POSTING CARD #:	234-07	AVERAGE WINNING TRADE OF THE DAY:	$ 585.52
LARGEST LOSING TRADE OF THE DAY:	$ (357.24)	LARGEST LOSING TRADE POSTING CARD #:	233-07	AVERAGE LOSING TRADE OF THE DAY:	$ (357.24)

111802　　　Copyright © 2002 by **TradersCoach.com, Inc.**

FIGURE 12.6 Student Daily Trade Ledger for September 6, 2007.

TradersCoach.com
"The Trader's Assistant"—A Trade Posting and Record Keeping System

TODAY'S DATE
SEPTEMBER 06, 07

DAILY WORKSHEET— Placed Orders

STATUS	TIME	SYMBOL	POSITION	SHARES	SIGNAL	PRICE $	FILL $	COMM $	POSTED	REMARKS
FILLED	7:18	ESU7	SHORT	2	PTP		1471.00	(3.62)	✓	
	7:39	ESU7	SHORT	2	SIO		1474.50	(3.62)	✓	
FILLED	9:22	ESU7	SHORT	4	BR2BR		1482.50	(14.48)	✓	
	9:50	ESU7	SHORT	4	CLO		1479.50	(14.48)	✓	

NOTES:

FIGURE 12.7 Student Daily Worksheet for September 6, 2007.

TRADE POSTING CARD EXAMPLES

Your trade posting cards are the front line of combat; this is where you will work to hold the line on profits with each and every trade. Do your best to record thoughts on entry and exit strategies and also feelings before opening the trade and after closing the trade.

It's impossible to capture accurate readings on your thoughts and feelings in hindsight, so try to get it on paper during the live trade. Following are a selection of a few actual student posting cards from the year, along with comments on what can be learned from each of them.

Trade Posting Card for January 4, 2007, $2009.14 Profit

Comments: This trade was one of the most profitable trades of the year, and the entry technique was effective. The exit technique consisted of scaling out of one-third of the position two times on reversal bar signals (see Figure 12.8 and Figure 12.9).

Trade Posting Card for January 23, 2007, $474.48 Loss

Comments: Here the student notes, "... This was not a very clever trade. I was influenced by the news ..." The trade was a short trade, and the charts were indicating a long position since the previous day. Here, trading psychology is tested and the television news influenced the short entry resulting in a loss (see Figure 12.10 and Figure 12.11).

Trade Posting Card for July 16, 2007, $243.10 Loss

Comments: The student notes, "... I did not execute this trade very well. I had 2 opportunities to scale out with one-bar reversal bars surrounding a double top. I could have posted a win instead of a loss. The question is: Am I greedy?" These are great notes and will be useful for going forward (see Figure 12.12 and Figure 12.13).

111802

TRADE POSTING CARD

☐ DAY TRADE ☒   ☐ POSITION TRADE

FUTURES   SYMBOL | N | Q | H | 7 | CLOSE DATE | 0 | 1 | – | 0 | 4 | – | 0 | 7 |

☐ LONG POSITION   ☒ SHORT POSITION

CARD# ___002 - 06___

TRADING TIME FRAME ___2-minute___

CONTRACT INFORMATION ___E-mini Nasdaq - 100___

☐ ASSET FOR OPTION   ☐ LONG TERM INVESTMENT   ☐ SHORT TERM SPECULATION   ☐ BOTTOM FISHING

BOUGHT

☐ OPEN   ☒ CLOSE

Contracts
1   11:49   1753.50
1   Price Per Contract $ 1756.25
1   11:23   1765.25   Amount Paid $ ___ (price per contract x # contracts)

Commission $ 1.81   1.81   1.81

Date | 0 | 1 | – | 0 | 3 | – | 0 | 7 | Time | 1 | 2 | : | 0 | 5 | AM/PM

TOTAL PAID $ ___
(amount paid + commission)

SOLD

☒ OPEN   ☐ CLOSE

Contracts ___3___   Price Per Contract $ ___1792.00___   Amount Recd $ ___ (price per contract x # contracts)

Commission $ 5.43

Date | 0 | 1 | – | 0 | 3 | – | 0 | 7 | Time | 1 | 0 | : | 4 | 9 | AM/PM

TOTAL RECD $ ___
(amount received - commission)

PROFIT/LOSS

Subtotal P/L $ ___2020.00___
(amount received - amount paid)

Total Commission $ ___<10.86>___
(bought comm + sold comm)

NET P/L $ ___2009.14___
(total received - total paid)

ACCOUNT

Brokerage ___   Account # ___

Copyright©2002   **TradersCoach.com, Inc.**

FIGURE 12.8   Student Trade Posting Card, Front, for January 4, 2007.

STOP-LOSS

DATE	TIME	SIGNAL	BUY/SELL	SHARES/CONTRACTS	PRICE	ACTUAL FILL
1-3-07	10:49	T/S	BUY	3	1797.50	
	11:06	T/S	BUY	3	1794.75	
	11:23	Scale Out ■	BUY	1		1765.25
	11:23	T/S	BUY	2	1794.75	$535 Profit
	11:39	T/S	BUY	2	1769.50	
	11:49	Scale Out ■	BUY	1		1753.50
	11:49	T/S	BUY	1	1769.50	$770 Profit
	12:05	CLO	BUY	1		1756.25

$715.00 Profit

$2020.00 Profit
Total

TRADING NOTES

FIGURE 12.9 Student Trade Posting Card, Back, for January 4, 2007.

TRADE POSTING CARD

111802

| 0 | 1 | – | 2 | 3 | – | 0 | 7 |

☒ DAY TRADE ☐ POSITION TRADE

FUTURES

SYMBOL | N | Q | H | 7

CLOSE DATE | 0 | 1 | – | 2 | 3 | – | 0 | 7

☐ LONG POSITION ☒ SHORT POSITION

TRADING TIME FRAME _2-minute_

CARD# _036 - 07_   CONTRACT INFORMATION _Nasdaq - 100 E-mini_

☐ ASSET FOR OPTION ☐ LONG TERM INVESTMENT ☐ SHORT TERM SPECULATION ☐ BOTTOM FISHING

BOUGHT   ☐ OPEN ☒ CLOSE

Contracts _4_   Price Per Contract $ _1794.25_   Amount Paid $ _____   Commission $ _7.24_
(price per contract x # contracts)

Date | 0 | 1 | – | 2 | 3 | – | 0 | 7   Time | 6 | : | 5 | 0 | AM/PM

TOTAL PAID $ _____
(amount paid + commission)

SOLD   ☒ OPEN ☐ CLOSE

Contracts _4_   Price Per Contract $ _1788.50_   Amount Recd $ _____   Commission $ _7.24_
(price per contract x # contracts)

Date | 0 | 1 | – | 2 | 3 | – | 0 | 7   Time | 6 | : | 4 | 0 | AM/PM

TOTAL RECD $ _____
(amount received - commission)

PROFIT/LOSS

Subtotal P/L $ _<460.00>_   Total Commission $ _<14.48>_   Total Commission $ _____
(amount received - amount paid)   (bought comm + sold comm)

NET P/L $ _<474.48>_
(total received - total paid)

ACCOUNT

Brokerage _____   Account # _____

Copyright©2002   TradersCoach.com, Inc.

FIGURE 12.10 Student Trade Posting Card, Front, for January 23, 2007.

STOP-LOSS

DATE	TIME	SIGNAL	BUY/SELL	SHARES/CONTRACTS	PRICE	ACTUAL FILL
1-22-07	6:40	T/S	BUY	4	1794.25	
	6:50	S/O	BUY	4		1794.25
						$(474.48)

TRADING NOTES

This was not a very clever trade. I was influenced by the news....When the chart was in an uptrend since yesterday

8:00 am. The 2' chart is too volatile. The 3' chart did not give me the bearish PTP

FIGURE 12.11 Student Trade Posting Card, Back, for January 23, 2007.

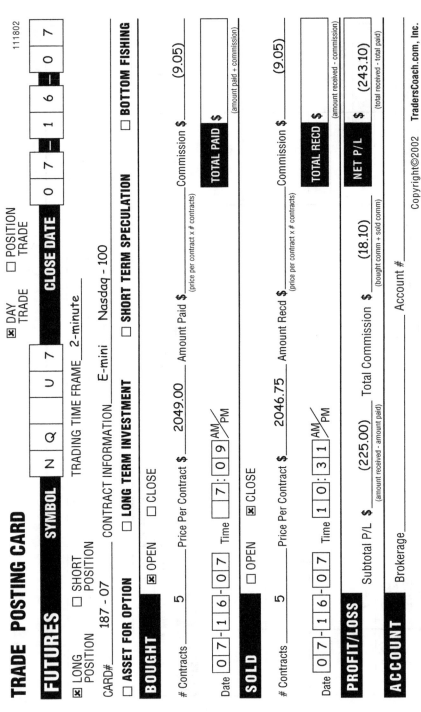

FIGURE 12.12 Trade Posting Card, Front, for July 16, 2007.

STOP-LOSS

DATE	TIME	SIGNAL	BUY/SELL	SHARES/CONTRACTS	PRICE	ACTUAL FILL
7-16-07	7:09	T/S	SELL	5	2046.75	
	10:31	S/O	SELL	5		2046.75

TRADING NOTES

I did not execute this trade very well. I had 2 opportunities to scale out with two 1-Bar Reversal Bars surrounding a double top. I could have posted a win instead of loss. The Question is: Am I Greedy?

FIGURE 12.13 Trade Posting Card, Back, for July 16, 2007.

Trade Posting Card for October 11, 2007, $1,451.64 Profit

Comments: The student notes, ". . . Market posted a bearish divergence between price and PO. Price reached Fibonacci Extension between 1.000 & 1.618 (n1586.75), which usually I have found to be a resistance. On the 5-minute chart a bearish Pyramid Trading Point was posted . . . this one was one of my best executions this year I think . . ." (See Figure 12.14 and Figure 12.15.)

THE ULTIMATE SCORECARD

The ultimate scorecard shows you what your profitability is by stating your win ratio and payoff ratio and more. See Figure 12.16 for a quick look at the annual scorecard of my trading students numbers. You will find it useful to keep a scorecard on your own performance. Use the scorecard form you will find in Appendix B.

PLOTTING YOUR EQUITY CURVE

It is useful to plot your equity curve to see how steady and smooth the growth is. The smoother your equity curve is the better. For our purposes we will briefly cover the topic of equity curve analysis so that you can see the value of plotting your actual numbers.

For a more in depth look at equity curve analysis, you will benefit from Tushar Chande's book *Beyond Technical Analysis, 2nd ed.*, Chapter 6. He goes into great detail about the SE or standard error aspect of your curve and how that can impact your profitability.

In Figure 12.17 you can see a perfectly smooth hypothetical example of an equity curve for a trading account that started with a $25,000 value on January 1, 2007. This graph has been drawn to show a hypothetical $1,000 increase in equity every month for 12 consecutive months. As you can see, the curve is actually a straight line that reaches from the bottom left corner to the upper right corner of the graph.

Tushar Chande would consider this equity curve to have an SE, standard error, value of 0 or zero because it is a perfectly smooth curve. In reality this curve would rarely, if ever, exist for a trader. A normal equity curve will ebb and flow like the market does, three steps forward, one step back and so on. What Chande explains is that the more ragged the equity curve

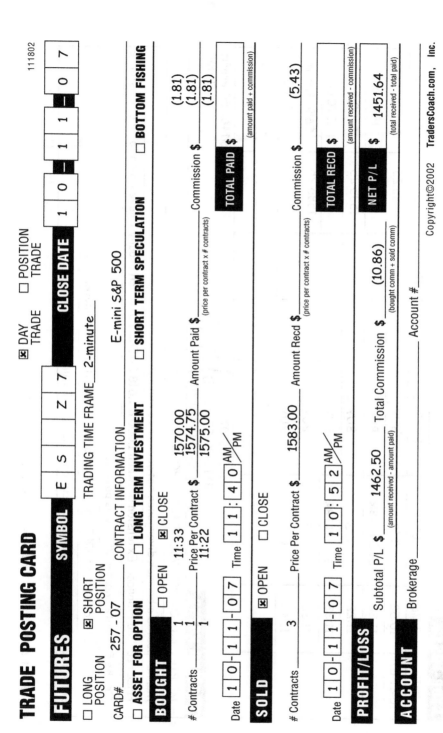

FIGURE 12.14 Student Trade Posting Card, Front, for October 11, 2007.

125

111802

STOP-LOSS

DATE	TIME	SIGNAL	BUY/SELL	SHARES/CONTRACTS	PRICE	ACTUAL FILL
10-11-07	10:52	T/S	BUY	3	1585.25	1575.00
	11:22	SCO BL1BR	BUY	1		$400 Profit
	11:22	T/S	BUY	2	1585.25	1570.00
	11:33	SCO BL1BR	BUY	1		$650 Profit
	11:33	T/S	BUY	1	1585.25	1574.00
	11:40	CLO	BUY	1		$412.50 Profit

A) 10-09-07 (10:44) } Fib Ext
B) 10-09-07 (13:04) } Points
B) 10-10-01 (10:30) }

$1462.50 Profit Total

TRADING NOTES

MP PTP : MINOR PYRAMID TRADING POINT

Market posted a bearish divergence between Price and PO.

Price reached Fibonacci Extension between 1.000 & 1.618 (~1586.75) which usually I have found to be a resistance.

On the 5-minute chart a ∇PTP was posted.

I close the trade after a BRPTP got voided out. Maybe not the best move. Will see.

But this one was one of my best executions this year, I think.

FIGURE 12.15 Student Trade Posting Card, Back, for October 11, 2007.

TRADING SCORE CARD

The Trader's Assistant By TradersCoach.com

Date: _____ 2007 _____

Circle One: Day   Week   Month   (Year)

Win Ratio:	39%
Payoff Ratio:	$ 1.96
Commission Ratio:	25%
Largest Winning Trade:	$ 2814.14
Largest Losing Trade:	$ (621.72)
Average Winning Trade:	$ 559.50
Average Losing Trade:	$ (285.59)
Largest % Of Draw Down:	12%
Average % Of Draw Down:	6%
Total % Of Profit / Loss:	50.7% Profit

FIGURE 12.16 Student Annual Scorecard for 2007 on a $25,000 paper trading account.

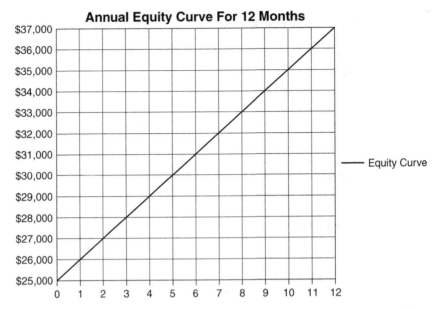

FIGURE 12.17 Perfectly Smooth Annual Equity Curve (Hypothetical Figures).

is, the less desirable it is. Therefore the goal is to minimize drawdowns as much as possible and maintain an even and steady curve upward.

On Figure 12.18 there is a more normal equity curve, more ragged than Figure 12.17. This graph shows you the equity curve my student plotted for the year 2007 for the paper trades he completed. Refer to Figure 12.1 to see his Annual Trade Ledger with running net profit and loss numbers which have been plotted on the Figure 12.18 graph. Here you can see graphically where the drawdowns occurred and where the winning periods occurred. It is a valuable exercise and once you have performance data you should plot your own numbers to create an illustration of your progress.

REAL-LIFE EXAMPLES ARE A STARTING POINT

These real-life examples from my trading student should give you a starting point to begin using your trading records in a way that will reveal otherwise invisible information. Capturing the information is the first goal, and knowing what to do with the information is the second goal. All in good time, the process will naturally unfold as you work through it.

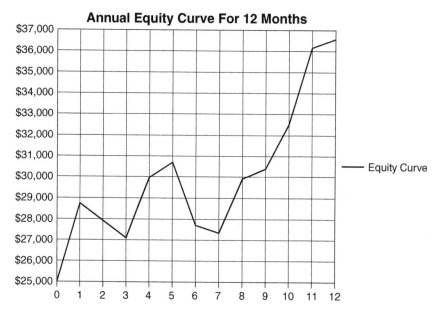

FIGURE 12.18 Student Annual Equity Curve (Year 2007 Results on a $25,000 paper trading account).

Remember, though my student is a day trader in the futures market you can still use this record keeping system if you are not a day trader and do not trade the futures market. The Trader's Assistant will work for you whether you are an investor, position trader, or a day trader. And, it works for any market you may be trading.

Annual Equity Curve For 12 Months

Design Your Own Plan

CHAPTER 13

Know Thyself—Your Risk Profile and Discipline Profile

K nowing yourself will enable you to operate more profitably in the financial markets. With that in mind, we want you to become introspective and identify what your risk profile and discipline profile are. These profile scores will assist you in customizing the best money management plan for you, which is covered in Chapter 14.

HOW COMFORTABLE ARE YOU WITH TAKING ON FINANCIAL RISK?

To know yourself and your risk tolerance is a valuable insight that can improve your money management system. Some traders have a greater appetite for risk than others. It is all relative, and that is why we need to understand our tendencies and our financial goals. It is also important to trade in our comfort zone.

On the one hand, if you are trading with too much risk for your tolerance level, you may increase your profit by reducing your stress and reducing your risk exposure. On the other hand, if you perform better with more risk, you may need to take that into consideration and make the necessary adjustments. It is all about knowing yourself and creating balance.

Your Risk Profile

We have developed a checklist and a scoring system to get you started on identifying your personal risk profile. This profile is designed to give you a guideline as to how much risk you are in a position to take on. It assesses what you feel your risk tolerance is, what risks you are currently exposed to, and what your skill level is. Answering these questions will give you your score:

1. What do you feel is the risk level of the market you trade or invest in? **(Your answer is based on your opinion.)**
   a. Low risk market, bonds, not using leverage, etc. (5 points)
   b. Medium risk market, stocks, etc. (10 points)
   c. High risk market, futures, using leverage, etc. (15 points)

2. What was the total percent of return on your active trading account over the last 12 months? (If you do not have 12 months of data, take your average percent per month and multiply it by 12)
   a. Up 50 percent or more over last 12 months (5 points)
   b. Up 10 to 50 percent over last 12 months (10 points)
   c. Lost money, or was up under 10 percent over last 12 months (15 points)

3. What is your average win ratio?
   a. 50 to 100 percent winning trades (5 points)
   b. 35 to 50 percent winning trades (10 points)
   c. 0 to 35 percent winning trades (15 points)

4. What do you feel is your personal risk tolerance? **(Your answer is based on your opinion.)**
   a. Prefer low-risk ventures (5 points)
   b. OK with medium-risk ventures (10 points)
   c. Enjoy high-risk ventures (15 points)

5. What is your trading experience level?
   a. Consistently profitable over 12-month period (5 points)
   b. Breaking even over 12-month period (10 points)
   c. No experience or losing consistently (15 points)

6. What is your average payoff ratio?
   a. Better than 3 to 1 (5 points)
   b. Between 2 to 1 and 3 to 1 (10 points)
   c. Worse than 2 to 1 (15 points)

Write Your Risk Score Here:_____

Once you have checked off one box for each of the six risk profile questions, then add up the number of total points and enter the score above. (You will see the points for each answer in parentheses next to your selection for each question.)

There is no good score or bad score; this is just a way to determine what will work best for your money management plan. You will come out with a score of 30 to 90 and your score will give you an idea of how to assess your risk management plan.

Risk Profile Score:

☐ **30–50 point score:** You are in a position to test taking on more risk, and it might be important to push the envelope on occasion and increase percent of capital at risk. If you have been risking 2 percent, you may try risking 3 percent or more if you are consistently profitable. If you do have a period of drawdown, immediately reduce your risk.

☐ **50–70 point score:** You are right on target and have an average risk profile. Steady as she goes.

☐ **70–90 point score:** You are in a position to take on less risk. Test reducing your percentage of capital at risk to see if it improves your bottom line. For example, if you are trading with 2 percent capital at risk, reduce to 1.5 percent. Watch out for overtrading. Reduce your risk percentage quickly the minute you experience drawdown.

HOW DISCIPLINED ARE YOU?

It is often said that traders cannot be consistently successful without being disciplined. This applies to both your money management system and to the discipline to carry out your trading plan. Often emotions can come into play, procrastination, fear, and anxiety. If you traditionally have difficulty with maintaining discipline and tend to be more of a spontaneous free thinker, you will need to focus on the plan and spontaneously stick to it.

Your Discipline Profile

Here we want to look at your personal tendencies to determine if you will need to work at being disciplined or if it will come more naturally. Again, we have a checklist with a score that will give you an idea of where you are on the spectrum:

1. Are you able to be punctual?
   a. Always on time (5 points)
   b. Sometimes on time (10 points)
   c. Never on time (15 points)

2. What is your diet like?
   a. Healthy and controlled (5 points)
   b. Don't really think about it (10 points)
   c. Unhealthy and uncontrolled (15 points)

3. Are you good with your record keeping and with keeping your check-book balanced?
   a. Always great at keeping records and analysis (5 points)
   b. Usually do record keeping (10 points)
   c. Sometimes do record keeping (15 points)

4. Do you have substantial clutter in your office?
   a. Never have clutter (5 points)
   b. Sometimes have clutter (10 points)
   c. Always have clutter (15 points)

5. Do you pay your bills and expenses on time?
   a. Always (5 points)
   b. Usually (10 points)
   c. Sometimes (15 points)

6. Have you got a regular exercise routine that you follow?
   a. Yes, I have a regular routine that I always follow (5 points)
   b. Yes, I have a regular routine that I sometimes follow (10 points)
   c. No, I have no routine (15 points)

Write Your Discipline Score Here:_____

Once you have checked off one box for each of the six discipline pro-file questions, then add up the number of total points and enter the score above. (You will see the points for each answer in parenthesis next to your selection for each question.)

There is no *good* score or *bad* score; this is just a way to determine what will work best for your money management plan. You will come out with a score of 30 to 90, and your score will give you an idea of how to set up your rules so that you take into account your discipline strengths or weaknesses.

Discipline Profile Score:

☐ **30–50 point score:** You are highly disciplined and will have the ability to easily follow your trading rules and maintain good record keeping. You are more of a left-brain thinker and will probably have some diffi-culty in thinking out of the box and coming up with creative solutions to trading challenges.

☐ **50–70 point score:** You are right on target and have an average discipline profile. You are more of a whole-brain thinker. Steady as she goes.

☐ **70–90 point score:** You generally struggle with being disciplined. You will need to really focus on keeping good records and analyzing your results. You are more of a right-brain thinker and will probably find it easier to come up with creative solutions to your trading challenges.

YOUR COMFORT ZONE

The two exercises in this chapter are intended to identify what your comfort zone is in regard to risk and discipline. The scores you came up with for your risk profile and discipline profile will help you design a custom plan that will serve you well. Use this knowledge to move your trading to the next level.

There are times when it pays to push the envelope and try to break out of our comfort zone. Trying new things and new ways of doing things can generate growth.

CHAPTER 14

Risk Management Rules to Choose From

N ow you're ready to design a custom money management system that suits your needs. When going through the following sets of rules, think about what your risk profile and discipline profile look like on paper. If you haven't yet completed those profiles, quickly go back to Chapter 13 and fill out the questions. Also, go to Chapter 3 to identify your strengths and weaknesses to see where you can address these personal attributes when designing your money management plan.

For example, if your risk profile determined that you have a score of 30, you may be able to "push the envelope" while designing your rules below and maybe increase the percentage of risk you take on each trade. However, if you have a score of 90, you may want to try to reduce the risk you take on each trade, which may improve your bottom line.

Regarding discipline, if you have a score of 30, you are highly disciplined. You'll probably have no difficulty following this plan once you complete it. For scores of 70 to 90, you may need to work a little on actually finishing the plan and then sticking to it. Visualize the benefits of completing this plan and profiting from the use of it, and then make the inner commitment to use it.

When you identify your current strengths and weaknesses, in Chapter 3, see how to play up your strengths and play down your weaknesses in your money management plan. All in all, knowing more about yourself will help you design a better plan that will generate greater profits.

YOU'VE GOT TO PLAY BY THE RULES!

You've got to play by the rules, your rules, that is. And you get to design your own plan and select the rules that work best for you. So roll up your sleeves and let's get to work.

We are going to break this down and tackle each area of the money management puzzle one step at a time. When we're done, you'll have a tailored system designed for your unique needs. It's probably a good idea to jot down notes as you work through this chapter so that you can edit and refine your plan. Start by checking off the boxes next to the rules that you feel will work best for you and your trading system.

As you go through the list of rules, remember that these rules are all relative. Each reader will have a completely different set of circumstances, so this list is designed to illustrate a concept. It is up to you to see how the concept either works for you or doesn't. This is why there is a box you can check off for "other." That way you can zero in on exactly what parameters suit you.

WHEN DO YOU GO ON HOLIDAY?

There comes a time when you will decide you are not trading well and it might not be immediately apparent as to why. For this reason, you may want to determine rules for deciding when to take a break from your trading and go on *holiday* for a bit. Here's a checklist of triggers you could choose to *stop* trading:

Remember, these are examples only. Choose your rules based on your personal trading results and style of trading.

In One Day

- ☐ 2 losing trades in a row
- ☐ 3 losing trades in a row
- ☐ $500 loss
- ☐ $1,000 loss
- ☐ Other:_____

In One Week

- ☐ 2 losing days in a row
- ☐ 3 losing days in a row
- ☐ $1,000 loss
- ☐ $2,000 loss
- ☐ Other:_____

In One Month

- ☐ 10% equity loss in your trading account
- ☐ Losing set of 25 trades (where after completing 25 consecutive trades you post a dollar loss for that period in your trading account)
- ☐ Other:_____

If you are experiencing a losing set of 25 trades (where after completing 25 consecutive trades you post a dollar loss for that period) or if you have a drawdown of greater than 15 percent in your account, which is unusual for you, it is important to stop trading. This is more than a holiday, and you will need to paper trade to find out what is the issue.

Is your psychology off? Are you not following your trading system rules? Have market conditions changed dramatically and your system is not adapting? Whatever it is, you need to get to the bottom of it and preserve your capital.

WHEN DO YOU TAKE THE MONEY AND RUN?

For some traders, it is best to take profit off the table when they reach a profit target. On occasion, traders will feel almost out of control when they have a large profit at stake. There can be a certain amount of anxiety with success, and if you feel that you have a tendency to *self-sabotage* you may want to create a holiday strategy for when you are doing well. Here are some ideas:

In One Day

- ☐ $500 profit
- ☐ $1,000 profit
- ☐ $2,000
- ☐ Other:_____

In One Week

- ☐ $1,000 profit
- ☐ $2,000 profit
- ☐ $5,000 profit
- ☐ Other:_____

With these holiday strategies, as you become more comfortable with a certain profit level, be sure to up the ante and increase your profit targets. Push yourself to grow and stretch your comfort zone.

HOW WILL YOU HANDLE DRAWDOWN?

Drawdown can affect both your trading psychology and your financial bottom line. Knowing yourself and how to approach periods of stop-outs and losses before they happen can enable you to lessen the negative effects. Following are some rules and ideas to start with. You may have many of your own rules and ideas that work for you; add them here as well:

☐ Ask the following questions on this checklist to analyze the drawdown:
  • Is this drawdown due to normal system probabilities?
  • Is this drawdown due to pilot error? Were there mistakes made, and what were they?
  • How can mistakes be avoided or reduced going forward?
  • Were all trading system rules followed?
  • Did you set a stop-loss exit prior to entering the trade?
  • Did you honor that stop-loss exit, or did you hesitate or delay?
  • Do any of the trading rules need to be adjusted going forward to reduce drawdown?
  • What is the percent of loss in the account?
  • Is this percent loss consistent with previous periods of drawdown?
  • What is the dollar amount of the loss in the account?
  • How many consecutive stop outs were incurred?
  • Other questions:_____

☐ When drawdown hits 10 percent of account value, reduce trade size and risk amount on each trade (refer to risk-of-ruin tables or use optimal f formula).

☐ When there are seven stop-outs in a row, reduce trade size and risk amount on each trade going forward (refer to risk-of-ruin tables or use the optimal f formula).

☐ When drawdown hits 15 percent of account value, stop live trading and begin paper trading until profitable again. Identify areas for improvement in prior trading and money management plans.

☐ When a lot of 25 consecutive trades produce a loss for that period, stop live trading and begin paper trading until profitable again. Identify areas for improvement in prior plans.

☐ Other:_____
☐ Other:_____

One important note about drawdown is that if after you paper trade and generate a paper profit you go into the live market and lose money, this means you have to work on your trading psychology. If you can generate profits in a practice environment but lose money in the live market your psychology is being affected by fear or some other emotion. Go back to Chapter 4 to see if you can identify the problem and correct it.

WHAT PERCENT OF YOUR TRADING ACCOUNT WILL YOU RISK ON EACH TRADE?

We've covered a couple of ways to determine what percentage of your trading account can be risked on any one trade. Very often, you will reduce your trade size and your risk exposure when you experience drawdown. Here you will identify what the best method is for doing that. Check off all of the following rules that apply:

- ☐ 2 percent maximum risk on each trade.
- ☐ Using my average monthly win ratio and payoff ratio, mathematically calculate optimal percent to risk using the optimal *f* formula for each new trade.
- ☐ Using my average monthly win ratio and payoff ratio, use the risk-of-ruin tables to find the best percentage to risk to give me a 0 percent probability of ruin for each new trade.
- ☐ After a drawdown, I will reduce the percent of risk by 25 percent. For example, if I am normally risking 2 percent on each trade, after a drawdown I will risk only 1.5 percent.
- ☐ Other:_____

WHAT TRADE SIZE WILL YOU USE?

When placing a trade, it all comes down to trade size. That's how you control your risk at your entry point. Following that, of course, is controlling your risk at the exit point. Determining your trade size is based on calculating your commission cost, entry, exit, and risk percent you will be using on any given trade.

Given that information, you can use your Trade Size Calculator to determine the number of contracts you will trade. Or, you can manually calculate the proper trade size using the formula in Chapter 10.

- ☐ Use Trade Size Calculator to determine proper trade size for every trade.
- ☐ Manually calculate proper trade size using formula in Chapter 10.
- ☐ Other:_____

WHAT PERCENT OF YOUR TRADING ACCOUNT WILL YOU RISK AT ANY GIVEN TIME?

The previous rule selections deal with per-trade risk percentages. This set of rule choices deals with your total percent of risk on the entire account. Again, you want to control the amount of total risk you sustain at any given point. If you have ten trades on all at once, each risking 2 percent, you are then putting 20 percent of your trading portfolio at risk, which may be too much risk for you. Here are some ideas for total account risk rules:

☐ 6 percent is the maximum active trading account risk. Example: You could have three live trades active, each with a separate risk of 2 percent.
☐ 10 percent is the maximum active trading account risk. Example: You could have five live trades active, each with a separate risk of 2 percent.
☐ Other:_____

WHAT PERCENT OF YOUR TOTAL NET WORTH WILL YOU RISK ON TRADING?

Most would agree that active trading involves more risk than investments. So, you will need to determine what your net worth is and what percent of that is realistic to put at risk in an active trading environment. My rule of thumb is generally not to risk more than 10 percent of one's net worth, but of course, if you are Bill Gates or Warren Buffett, you can safely risk much more than 10 percent. So here you will determine what the right amount is for you. As your net worth grows, you can reevaluate the amount you have in your trading account.

☐ 10 percent of total net worth is the maximum amount risked in my active trading account.
☐ Other:_____

WHEN WILL YOU EXIT A TRADE?

Identifying exits really falls under the trading system category in that your exits should be placed at meaningful places in the market that are determined by support and resistance. With that said, it is important to always determine your initial exit *prior* to entering the trade. And then you need to exit your trade when your stop tells you to.

Seems simple enough, but in reality, it can be emotionally difficult to achieve, depending on how the trade is going and how developed your trading psychology is. Refer to Chapter 7 for more details on designing your rules. Here are some to start with:

☐ Determine initial stop-loss exit prior to entering the trade.
☐ Adhere to stop-loss exit when it is hit, and exit the market immediately.
☐ Use a stop-loss exit strategy that is based on market price activity, key support and resistance levels, volume, volatility dynamics, and/or on fundamental rules (not on random and spontaneous decisions).
☐ Use trailing stops to lock in profit when the market moves in your favor.
☐ Use scaling-out rules (see next section) to lock in profit and relieve anxiety.
☐ Do not move stops for emotional reasons.
☐ When you increase your trade size (by scaling in to a position), adjust your stop to allow for additional risk.
☐ When holding a position overnight, if you are a day trader, adjust your stop to allow for additional overnight risk.
☐ Try to have stops that breathe so that you do not get whipsawed when the market is choppy.
☐ Other:_____

HOW WILL YOU SCALE OUT OF A POSITION?

Scaling out of positions can be a great way to lock in profit and reduce anxiety when a position has a sharp turn into profitable territory. Identify the rules you want to use in determining when to scale out. Some ideas for these rules could be:

☐ 30 percent for first scale-out, 30 percent for second scale-out, and hold 40 percent of trade until getting stopped out.
☐ 1/3 of position for first scale-out, 1/3 of position for second scale-out and hold the remaining 1/3 until stopped out.
☐ When market gaps in a profitable direction creating a 50 percent gain. Example: If you entered a long stock position at $20.00 per share and it gapped up to $30.00 per share, you could liquidate a portion of your position to lock in profit.
☐ Other:_____

HOW WILL YOU SCALE IN TO A POSITION?

Scaling in to a position will increase your trade size and will increase your risk. When doing this you must carefully balance your risk-to-reward probabilities. Consider the following rules:

- ☐ Only scale in to a winning position.
- ☐ Do not double down.
- ☐ When you scale in to a position, recalculate your risk based on the new trade size and stop-loss exit.
- ☐ Other:_____

HOW WILL YOU DIVERSIFY?

Diversification is crucial in managing your risk. There are a number of ways to do this. It requires that you diversify all of your accounts, both investment and active trading. It also means that you do not invest or trade all of your account in the company that you are employed by. The possible risk of this is losing everything including your job, your investments, and your retirement plan, which is what happened to Enron share holders (who were also employees) that had virtually no diversification. Rule number one, do not "put all your eggs in one basket," so if that basket drops, it is only a small portion of your holdings that are lost.

- ☐ 2 percent per sector can be risked at any give time. Example: If you have a total of 6 percent of your trading account at risk, you could have 2 percent in the technology sector, 2 percent in the energy sector, and 2 percent in the currency sector.
- ☐ Other:_____

ESTABLISH YOUR RECORD KEEPING RULES

Record keeping is essential in furthering your progress and profitability in trading. This means you have to have the commitment to run the numbers every day you trade. Not every other day or once a month, but every day. Refer to Chapters 11 and 12 to find out more about record keeping. Here's a start of some rules to follow:

- ☐ Track every single trade every day.
- ☐ Write down the entry and exit price, and calculate the profit/loss.

☐ Write down your emotions and feelings prior to, during, and after the trade is completed.

☐ Tabulate all totals for every day, week, month, and year of trades.

☐ Analyze totals at the end of each period, day week, month, and year.

☐ Determine adjustments that may improve performance for both your money management system and trading system based on the facts (not based on any distortions—avoiding the tabulation of totals can lead to distortions—so be sure to run the numbers).

☐ Fill out your scorecard so that you know what is your win ratio; payoff ratio; commission ratio; largest winning trade and largest losing trade; average winning trade and average losing trade; largest number of consecutive losses; average number of consecutive losses; largest trading account drawdown; average trading account drawdown; and percent of profit or loss on account each and every period.

☐ Other:_____

WRITE IT DOWN

Take the rules that you have designed for yourself and write them down. Type them into your computer, hand-write them in a notebook—whatever works for you. The process of writing your rules down will rewire your brain with this new information (or modified old information from an existing plan) and will make the pathways more clear.

Now the minute you have drawdown, your brain knows what to do. You know what your scaling out rules are, your rules for risk percent on each trade, trade size rules, and so on. Write it down now, since this step is important. It is the step where you make the commitment to follow the money management system you just designed, and you are telling your brain what the plan is.

Epilogue

My plan is that *A Trader's Money Management System* will simplify some otherwise complicated information in a way that will make is easy for you to implement. And once implemented, my hope is that you will generate greater profits than you ever did before by executing a well-thought-out risk control plan.

Money management has become one of my favorite parts of trading, and the dream is that this book may popularize this area of study and "make it sexy" to a point where it is something most everyone enjoys working on. My idea is to spell out each step very simply and clearly so that you can instantly know, step by step and formula by formula, what you need to do.

The mathematical formulas in this book are not incredibly difficult to implement, but I think in the past many traders have been intimidated by the mathematical complexities of trading and money management. I'd like to change that for as many traders as possible—take away the fear and intimidation of the math.

I think the key is to start with the essentials. When you have the foundation of your plan laid out, you can explore some of the more complicated aspects (mathematical and otherwise) using the books that are listed in the resources section. Once you've mastered the basics of money management, you can always take it to the next level.

May you happily manage your risk, embrace your risk, and not fear your risk for the rest of your trading career.

BENNETT A. MCDOWELL
San Diego, California
March 2008

Getting Started with Your Trade Size Calculator Software

A 30-Day Trade Size Calculator Download

T his book comes with a 30-day free trial of the Trade Size Calculator. The 30-day period does not begin and your Trade Size Calculator software does not become activated until you register your software on the TradersCoach.com Web site. Upon completing your 30-day trial, you are entitled to discounted rates on this software lease and ownership options.

Once you have registered your software, your e-mail technical support will begin. It is important to understand that this 30-day trial is a very special free offer, which means that technical support will be limited to *e-mail support only*. Additional support services are available from www.traderscoach.com for an additional fee if you require more assistance. Please call us or visit the Web site for more information.

Also, the e-mail technical support that you receive for 30 days is designed to troubleshoot technical issues only. For trading and investing methodology issues, refer to *A Trader's Money Management System*, which, if studied, will answer your questions in detail.

How to Register Your Software

Log on to www.traderscoach.com and click on the icon that has the cover of this book. It will give you all the information you need.

Technical Support

Again, *technical support for the Trade Size Calculator software is available via e-mail only.* We provide telephone support, but please understand that our telephone representatives are trained to answer general questions only and are not able to provide technical support.

Technical Email Support: 24 hours per day/7 days per week; e-mail your detailed questions to support@traderscoach.com.

    Depending on the volume of e-mails we receive, your e-mail will be responded to in a time period from 1 hour to 24 hours from the receipt of your request. Support is given on a first-come, first-served basis. (Occasionally, our technical support volume is huge; we appreciate your patience during these times.) To ensure the best possible technical response, please make sure your e-mails are detailed and clear.

General Telephone Support: 24 hours per day/7 days per week; call us at 1 (858) 695–0592.

The Trader's Assistant Record Keeping System

Included in this appendix are all The Trader's Assistant, by Traders Coach.com, blank forms, trade posting cards, and trade ledgers. You can photocopy and start using them right from the book. When you photocopy the pages from this book, you will want to enlarge them to fit the final layout size.

It is best to three-hole punch the ledgers so that you can put them into a binder. The trade posting cards work best printed on index stock; your local copy shop should be able to cut them to size for you. We've indicated what the final layout sizes are for both the ledgers and the cards.

Here is a list of the forms included:

1. Annual Trade Ledger, front, Figure B.1 (final size is 8 1/2″ × 11″)
2. Monthly Trade Ledger, front, Figure B.2 (final size is 8 1/2″ × 11″)
3. Weekly Trade Ledger, front, Figure B.3 (final size is 8 1/2″ × 11″)
4. Daily Trade Ledger, front, Figure B.4 (final size is 8 1/2″ × 11″)
5. Daily Worksheet, front, Figure B.5 (final size is 8 1/2″ × 11″)
6. All Ledgers, back, Figure B.6 (final size is 8 1/2″ × 11″)
7. Futures Trade Posting Card, front, Figure B.7 (final size 8″ × 5″)
8. Stocks Trade Posting Card, front, Figure B.8 (final size 8″ × 5″)
9. Options Trade Posting Card, front, Figure B.9 (final size 8″ × 5″)
10. All Posting Cards, back, Figure B.10 (final size 8″ × 5″)
11. Trading Scorecard Figure B.11.

TradersCoach.com
"The Trader's Assistant"—A Trade Posting and Record Keeping System

YEAR OF LEDGER

ANNUAL TRADE LEDGER

MONTH	# TRADES	# WINNING	# LOSING	GROSS $ P/L	COMMISSION $	NET $ P/L	RUNNING NET $ P/L
JANUARY							
FEBRUARY							
MARCH							
APRIL							
MAY							
JUNE							
JULY							
AUGUST							
SEPTEMBER							
OCTOBER							
NOVEMBER							
DECEMBER							
TOTALS:							

| LARGEST WINNING TRADE OF THE YEAR: | $ | LARGEST WINNING TRADE POSTING CARD #: | | AVERAGE WINNING TRADE OF THE YEAR: | $ |
| LARGEST LOSING TRADE OF THE YEAR: | $ | LARGEST LOSING TRADE POSTING CARD #: | | AVERAGE LOSING TRADE OF THE YEAR: | $ |

NOTES:

111802

FIGURE B.1 Annual Trade Ledger, front, The Trader's Assistant, by TradersCoach.com.

TradersCoach.com
"The Trader's Assistant" — A Trade Posting and Record Keeping System

MONTH OF LEDGER

MONTHLY TRADE LEDGER

WEEK	# TRADES	# WINNING	# LOSING	GROSS $ P/L	COMMISSION $	NET $ P/L	RUNNING NET $ P/L
1							
2							
3							
4							
5							
TOTALS:							

LARGEST WINNING TRADE OF THE MONTH:	$	LARGEST WINNING TRADE POSTING CARD #:	AVERAGE WINNING TRADE OF THE MONTH:	$
LARGEST LOSING TRADE OF THE MONTH:	$	LARGEST LOSING TRADE POSTING CARD #:	AVERAGE LOSING TRADE OF THE MONTH:	$

NOTES: ....
....
....
....
....
....
....
....
....
....
....

FIGURE B.2 Monthly Trade Ledger, front, The Trader's Assistant, by TradersCoach.com.

TradersCoach.com
"The Trader's Assistant"— A Trade Posting and Record Keeping System

WEEKLY TRADE LEDGER

DAY	# TRADES	# WINNING	# LOSING	GROSS $ P/L	COMMISSION $	NET $ P/L	RUNNING NET $ P/L
MONDAY							
TUESDAY							
WEDNESDAY							
THURSDAY							
FRIDAY							
SATURDAY							
SUNDAY							
TOTALS:							

LARGEST WINNING TRADE OF THE WEEK: $	LARGEST WINNING TRADE POSTING CARD #:	AVERAGE WINNING TRADE OF THE WEEK: $
LARGEST LOSING TRADE OF THE WEEK: $	LARGEST LOSING TRADE POSTING CARD #:	AVERAGE LOSING TRADE OF THE WEEK: $

NOTES: ....

....

....

....

....

FIGURE B.3 Weekly Trade Ledger, front, The Trader's Assistant, by TradersCoach.com.

TradersCoach.com
"The Trader's Assistant" — A Trade Posting and Record Keeping System

TODAY'S DATE

DAILY TRADE LEDGER — Filled Orders

Open Position Trades Carried Forward

POSITION TRADE NUMBER	POSTING CARD NUMBER	SYMBOL	POSITION	SHARES	BOUGHT $	SOLD $	GROSS $ P/L	COMM $	NET $ P/L	RUNNING NET $ P/L
1										
2										
3										
4										
5										
POSITION TRADE TOTALS						⟶				

New Trades Filled Today

TODAY'S TRADE NUMBER	POSTING CARD NUMBER	SYMBOL	POSITION	SHARES	BOUGHT $	SOLD $	GROSS $ P/L	COMM $	NET $ P/L	RUNNING NET $ P/L
1										
2										
3										
4										
5										
6										
7										
8										
9										
10										
DAY TRADE TOTALS						⟶				
GRAND TOTALS						⟶				

LARGEST WINNING TRADE OF THE DAY:	$	LARGEST WINNING TRADE POSTING CARD #:		AVERAGE WINNING TRADE OF THE DAY:	$
LARGEST LOSING TRADE OF THE DAY:	$	LARGEST LOSING TRADE POSTING CARD #:		AVERAGE LOSING TRADE OF THE DAY:	$

111802

FIGURE B.4 Daily Trade Ledger, front, The Trader's Assistant, by TradersCoach.com.

TradersCoach.com
"The Trader's Assistant"— A Trade Posting and Record Keeping System

TODAY'S DATE

DAILY WORKSHEET— Placed Orders

STATUS	TIME	SYMBOL	POSITION	SHARES	SIGNAL	PRICE $	FILL $	COMM $	POSTED	REMARKS

NOTES:

Copyright © 2002 by **TradersCoach.com,Inc.**

FIGURE B.5 Daily Worksheet, front, The Trader's Assistant, by TradersCoach.com.

TradersCoach.com
"The Trader's Assistant" — A Trade Posting and Record Keeping System

TRADING NOTES

(blank ruled lines)

STANDARD ABBREVIATIONS FOR TRADING TERMS

Use these quick shorthand abbreviations on your "Trade Posting Cards" and "Trade Ledgers".

Add any additional abbreviations that you find helpful.

Add-On	A/O
Break-Out	B/O
Closed	CLO
Commission	COM
Covered Call	C/C
Dollar	$
End-Of-Day	EOD
Expired	EXP
Future	FUT
Market	MKT
Naked	NKD
Opened	OPN
Option	OPT
Premium	PRE
Roll Over	R/O
Signal	SIG
Spread	SPD
Stop Loss	S/L
Stopped Out	S/O
Support	SUP
Trading Error	T/E
Trailing Stop	T/S
Underlying Asset	U/A

111802

FIGURE B.6 All Ledgers, back, The Trader's Assistant, by TradersCoach.com.

TRADE POSTING CARD

111802

□ DAY TRADE □ POSITION TRADE

FUTURES **SYMBOL**

□ LONG POSITION □ SHORT POSITION

CLOSE DATE ___

CARD# ___

TRADING TIME FRAME ___

CONTRACT INFORMATION ___

□ ASSET FOR OPTION □ LONG TERM INVESTMENT □ SHORT TERM SPECULATION □ BOTTOM FISHING

BOUGHT

□ OPEN □ CLOSE

Contracts ___ Price Per Contract $ ___ Amount Paid $ ___ Commission $ ___
(price per contract x # contracts)

Date [ ] [ ] - [ ] [ ] Time [ ] [ ] : [ ] [ ] □ AM □ PM

TOTAL PAID $ ___
(amount paid + commission)

SOLD

□ OPEN □ CLOSE

Contracts ___ Price Per Contract $ ___ Amount Rec'd $ ___ Commission $ ___
(price per contract x # contracts)

Date [ ] [ ] - [ ] [ ] Time [ ] [ ] : [ ] [ ] □ AM □ PM

TOTAL REC'D $ ___
(amount received - commission)

PROFIT/LOSS

Subtotal P/L $ ___ Total Commission $ ___ **NET P/L $** ___
(amount received - amount paid) (bought comm + sold comm) (total received - total paid)

ACCOUNT

Brokerage ___ Account # ___

To reorder cards: Email your order to **TradersCoach.com**, or call (858) 695-1985. Copyright©2002 **TradersCoach.com, Inc.**

FIGURE B.7 Futures Trade Posting Card, front, The Trader's Assistant, by TradersCoach.com.

TRADE POSTING CARD

111802

STOCKS

SYMBOL

☐ DAY TRADE ☐ POSITION TRADE

CLOSE DATE

☐ LONG POSITION ☐ SHORT POSITION

TRADING TIME FRAME _____

CARD# _____

COMPANY NAME _____

☐ ASSET FOR OPTION ☐ LONG TERM INVESTMENT ☐ SHORT TERM SPECULATION ☐ BOTTOM FISHING

BOUGHT

☐ OPEN ☐ CLOSE

Shares _____ Price Per Share $ _____ Amount Paid $ _____ Commission $ _____

(price per share x shares)

Date ☐-☐☐-☐ Time ☐☐:☐☐ AM/PM

TOTAL PAID $ _____

(amount paid + commission)

SOLD

☐ OPEN ☐ CLOSE

Shares _____ Price Per Share $ _____ Amount Recd $ _____ Commission $ _____

(price per share x shares)

Date ☐-☐☐-☐ Time ☐☐:☐☐ AM/PM

TOTAL RECD $ _____

(amount received - commission)

PROFIT/LOSS

Subtotal P/L $ _____ Total Commission $ _____

(amount received - amount paid) (bought comm + sold comm)

NET P/L $ _____

(total received - total paid)

ACCOUNT

Brokerage _____ Account # _____

To reorder cards: Email your order to **TradersCoach.com**, or call (858) 695-1985.

Copyright©2002 **TradersCoach.com, Inc.**

FIGURE B.8 Stocks Trade Posting Card, front, The Trader's Assistant, by TradersCoach.com.

161

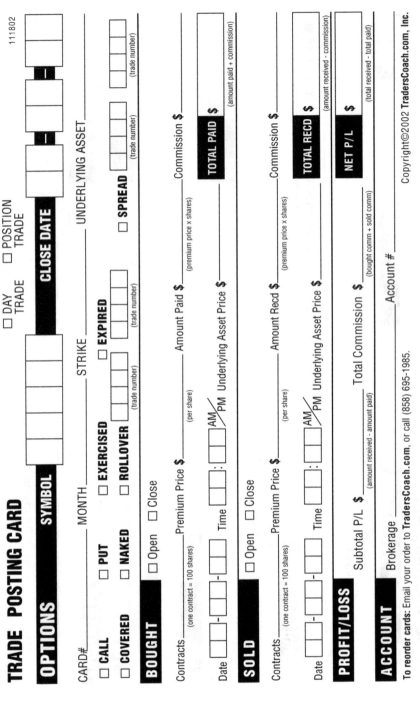

FIGURE B.9 Options Trade Posting Card, front, The Trader's Assistant, by TradersCoach.com.

STOP-LOSS

111802

DATE	TIME	SIGNAL	BUY/SELL	SHARES/CONTRACTS	PRICE	ACTUAL FILL

TRADING NOTES

To reorder cards: Email your order to TradersCoach.com, or call (858) 695-1985.

FIGURE B.10 All Posting Cards, back, The Trader's Assistant, by TradersCoach.com.

TRADING SCORE CARD

The Trader's Assistant By TradersCoach.com

Date: _____

Circle One: Day   Week   Month   Year

_____

Win Ratio:

_____

Payoff Ratio:

_____

Commission Ratio:

_____

Largest Winning Trade:

_____

Largest Losing Trade:

_____

Average Winning Trade:

_____

Average Losing Trade:

_____

Largest % Of Draw Down:

_____

Average % Of Draw Down:

_____

Total % Of Profit / Loss:

_____

FIGURE B.11   Trading Scorecard, The Trader's Assistant, by TradersCoach.com.

SETTING UP YOUR RECORD KEEPING SYSTEM

We've designed the Trader's Assistant system so that you can set it up in an organized way. In order to do this we recommend you purchase the following items at your local office supply store:

- Two three-ring binders, size 3-inch spine, for "workbook" and "yearbook"
- Two file card boxes, size 8″ × 5″ for "open trades" and "closed trades"
- Tab divider set with January to December tabs for "yearbook" three-ring binder
- Tab divider set with five blank tabs for "workbook" three-ring binder
- File card divider set with January to December tabs for 8″ × 5″ file box "closed trades"
- File card divider set with A to Z alphabetized tabs for 8″ × 5″ file box "open trades"

You will want to purchase at least two three-ring binders to file your trade ledgers. The first binder will be called your "yearbook" and the second binder will be called your "workbook."

For the yearbook, you need tab dividers; have sections for each month January to December. The workbook will need five blank tab dividers:

1. Daily worksheets
2. Daily trade ledgers
3. Weekly trade ledgers
4. Monthly trade ledgers
5. Annual trade ledger

As you complete each month in your workbook, you will want to transfer the record for that month into the yearbook.

Label the two file boxes, one as "open trades" and one as "closed trades." Put the A to Z tab dividers into the *open trade* box. Put the January to December dividers into the *closed trade* box.

You will be filing your open trade posting cards alphabetically by the first letter of the market *symbol*, which you will fill in at the top of each card. When the trade is closed and you have posted a profit or loss, you will then file the card in your closed trade box behind the tab divider for the appropriate month, based on the *close date*, which you will fill in at the top right of each card.

ADAPT THE TRADER'S ASSISTANT SYSTEM TO SUIT YOUR NEEDS

The outline we've given you on how to set up the system is a starting point. Of course, you should adapt it in any way that will make it more effective for you. Some students like to print the trade posting cards on one sheet of paper, with the front of the card at the top and the back of the card at the bottom of the sheet. Then they can put them into a three-ring binder along with all the ledgers.

Remember, I designed this system for myself and my preferences, and I like to use the index card approach. The main goal is that you capture your statistical and historical information. Plus, don't forget to capture both the psychological feelings and the profit/loss statistics. How you achieve the end result is up to you. We're just giving you a starting point.

THE TRADER'S ASSISTANT FORMS ARE ALSO AVAILABLE IN A PDF FILE FORMAT

If you would prefer to duplicate the forms in this book from a PDF file you can download the file from the TradersCoach.com Web site for a nominal fee. In addition, all of the forms and the complete system are also available from TradersCoach.com for purchase. We would be happy to help you with any of your record keeping needs, feel free to contact us at the TradersCoach.com Web site or call us via: www.TradersCoach.com 858–695-0592.

The Art of
Paper Trading

I t's beneficial to be profitable first by *paper trading* before trading with real money. Although paper trading will not have exactly the same psychological feel as trading with real money, it is a useful way to practice your trading skills in a stress-free environment so that you can focus on your financial approach and trading rules. Paper trading gives you time to hone your trading skills without losing money.

Those of you who are my students or have read my book, *The ART®️ of Trading*, already know my position in favor of paper trading. Ironically, this topic is frequently debated, and there are a few traders who have gone on record as opposing the entire idea of paper trading. We'll go into the pros and cons of the subject in the following pages.

EVERY FINANCIAL MARKET IS A CHAMPIONSHIP ARENA

Trading is a zero-sum game. When you enter any financial market you will be competing against some very skilled professionals. If you enter the market as a novice, you will be competing against traders who have more skill, more experience, and a larger account size. To give yourself a fighting chance, you need to enter the markets as skilled as a professional. Anything less will make it impossible to succeed in trading on a consistent basis.

The best way to develop your trading skills is by paper trading, which allows you to practice without the pressure of losing money. If you cannot even be profitable paper trading, how on earth do you plan to be profitable trading with real money and more stress?

As I mentioned earlier, some traders believe that paper trading is useless because you won't feel the psychological emotions that are experienced when trading with real money. I strongly disagree with this. In the beginning, you will find that, surprisingly enough, paper trading creates a similar emotional roller coaster as trading with real money—that is, if you approach paper trading with the same dedication.

The deeper psychological and emotional aspects of trading your hard-earned money can be worked on later, after you have developed your trading skills. It is first better to have your approach developed through paper trading and then work on developing a deeper trading psychology over time.

Don't be impatient with your paper trading. Allow yourself time to develop your trading skills and approach. This is time very well spent, so no short-cuts here.

PAPER TRADING TEN-STEP PLAN

1. **Design your trading rules and your money management rules.** After you have designed both your trading rules (either technical, fundamental, or a combination of the two), then write them down on paper in a checklist format. Cover every aspect of your entries, exits, and overall methodology. In addition, get your money management rules written down in the same way.

2. **Start to paper trade.** Once you are clear on your rules, start paper trading on the same time frame, financial market, and with the account size you plan to work with when you use real money.

   If you have the time to day trade, it is best for you to paper trade your favorite market. Day trading will shorten your learning curve because you will trade more often and gain more experience for a given period of time.

   See if trend trading, scalping, scaling in or scaling out suits you. Through trial and error in a safe, paper-trading environment, you will be able to determine if you need to adapt your rules.

3. **Evaluate your performance**. Keep track of your paper trading results and approach this as if you are trading with real money. Use the Trader's Assistant Record Keeping System (see Chapter 12).

4. **Group in lots of 25 trades.** Group your paper trades in lots of 25 trades each, and calculate your profit/loss, average win/loss, largest win/loss, number of winning trades, number of losing trades, and number of consecutive winning and losing trades. A group of 25 consecutive trades that has a profitable outcome is a profitable lot.

5. **Practice until profitable.** Analyze your trading results and make adjustments until you are profitable, and feel good about your trading.

6. **Three consecutive profitable lots of 25 trades.** Before trading with real money, be sure you have a total of three profitable consecutive lots of 25 trades each while paper trading. If you're a day trader, be sure to have spread your day trading over enough days, weeks, or months so you experience up trending, down trending, and bracketed markets.

7. **Keep trading in lots of 25 trades.** When trading with real money, keep using the 25 trade-lot size to analyze your profit/loss, and so on, and see how you are doing.

8. **Reevaluate your approach.** If you are not profitable trading with real money after trading one lot of 25 trades, stop trading and go back to paper trading.

   If you are then immediately profitable paper trading, then chances are your psychology is the problem and you may need some additional help from a trading coach to uncover your psychological sabotage issues.

   If your paper trading is not immediately profitable this time, then you may have just been lucky the first time you paper traded and did not do it long enough to experience the different types of market cycles. Your trading approach needs to be adjusted.

   Until you have a qualified trading approach as proven through how you paper trade, then you will not know if you problem lies in your trading approach or if your problem is with your psychology.

9. **Experiencing losses.** If you experience six consecutive losing trades and/or a drawdown of more than 15 percent, the market cycle or volatility on the market and time frame you are trading has probably changed. You must adapt quickly and effectively to these changes.

10. **During excessive drawdown, follow these steps.**

    a. Stop trading with real money. Keep trading the same market and time frame and go back to paper trading. Wait until you have three winning lots of 25 paper trades before trading with real money again.

    b. Make adjustments to your rules to see if that eliminates the losses you incurred in your recent drawdown. If so, paper trade again to validate your adjustments.

   c. Change time frames until you find the time frame that is working the best.

PAPER TRADING IS FOR SISSIES!

Getting back to the traders who feel paper trading is not beneficial—it seems valuable at this time to address the most common objections to a paper trading approach. Here are the ones I hear the most:

1. **Paper trading doesn't subject you to the same emotions.** You know, that may be true to a point, yet it doesn't seem intelligent to use that as an argument. In medical school, would it make sense for surgeons to operate on live patients before they really know what they are doing? Don't think so. Trading is a life and death situation—your financial life and death, that is. Treat it with the respect it deserves and paper trade until you know what you are doing.

2. **You'll get addicted to paper trading.** I guess there are people who feel they'll be afraid to pull the trigger if they paper trade too long. Here's the thing: If you know that your plan says you will have three sets of consecutive trades (25 in each set) that are profitable sets before you go live with real money, why be afraid to pull the trigger? If you prove to yourself you can be profitable, there is no problem. Then if you prove to yourself you can't be profitable, you better fix the problem.

3. **Back testing is the only way to test a system.** There are lots of ways to back test. In essence, paper trading is one of the ways you can back test. eSignal has a great playback feature where you can take data from the day (or week or month or year) and play it back. You can, in a sense, paper trade a live market. Granted, technically it is not live, but if you play it forward one price bar at a time, you will feel as if you are trading it live. The value of testing your system in this way is that you are not only testing your system rules, you are testing your emotions and ability to follow those rules.

4. **It's too much work.** Yes, it requires dedication and work to complete three sets of 25 profitable trades. But then again, anything of real value usually requires some work. The value acquired from this type of paper trading produces results. I've seen it time and again. The question is, are you under the illusion that trading profits will be quick and easy? And, if you enjoy the actual process of your trading, it won't seem like work since every step of progress will give you great satisfaction.

5. **Paper trading is for sissies.** Well, no one has ever really said that to me, but the implication is there. You know, real men don't paper trade (or eat quiche). The reality is that paper trading is an effective way to hone your skills in the market and it is not something to shy away from.

WHAT DO YOU THINK ABOUT PAPER TRADING?

All that matters right now is, what do you think about paper trading? My sincere hope is that you see the benefit and will implement a plan to test your rules and see how they hold up prior to putting your money on the line.

For the more advanced traders who already know from experience they have a winning system, keep an open mind and paper trade through any challenging drawdowns. Test a new trading idea or approach and paper trade it to see if your drawdown might be the catalyst for a new way of trading.

Resources

BOOK AND VIDEO SOURCES

Amazon.com
www.amazon.com

Traders Press
www.traderspress.com
1-800-927-8222
1-864-298-0222

Traders Library
www.traderslibrary.com
1-800-272-2855
1-410-964-0026

RECOMMENDED BOOKS

Balsara, Nauzer. *Money Management Strategies for Futures Traders.* John Wiley & Sons, 1992.

Chande, Tushar. *Beyond Technical Analysis: How to Develop and Implement a Winning Trading System, 2nd ed.*, John Wiley & Sons, 2001.

McDowell, Bennett. *The ART® of Trading: Combining the Science of Technical Analysis with the Art of Reality Based Trading.* John Wiley & Sons, 2008.

Vince, Ralph. *Portfolio Management Formulas: Mathematical Trading Methods for the Futures, Options, and Stock Markets.* John Wiley & Sons, 1990.

PERIODICALS

Technical Analysis of Stocks and Commodities
www.traders.com
1-800-832-4642
1-206-938-0570
13 issues per year
$64.95 USD cost per year

Traders World
www.tradersworld.com
1-800-288-4266
1-417-882-9697
4 issues per year
$19.95 USD cost per year

Futures **Magazine**
www.futuresmag.com
1-800-458-1734
1-847-763-9252
11 issues per year
$68.00 USD cost per year

Active Trader
www.activetradermag.com
1-800-341-9384
1-312-775-5421
12 issues per year
$59.40 USD cost per year

SFO (Stocks, Futures And Options)
www.sfomag.com
1-800-590-0919
1-319-268-0441
12 issues per year

IBD (Investor's Business Daily)
www.investors.com
1-800-831-2525
1-310-448-6600

250 issues per year
$295.00 USD cost per year

The Wall Street Journal
www.wsj.com
1-800-568-7625
360 issues per year
$249.00 USD cost per year

Barron's
www.barronsmag.com
1-800-568-7625
45 issues per year
$179.00 USD cost per year

EDUCATION

TradersCoach.com: TradersCoach.com, founded in 1998 by Bennett A. McDowell, is a worldwide leader in trader education and support. Dedicated to providing a no-nonsense and honest approach to trading and investing in the financial markets, TradersCoach.com has impeccable integrity and is a member of the Better Business Bureau's online network.

The products and services offered include free monthly educational webcasts, the *ART (Applied Reality Trading)* technical analysis software, the Trader's Assistant record-keeping system, and the Trade Size Calculator software. In addition, Bennett McDowell offers private coaching and consultations to traders around the world to give them the support they need on a variety of subjects from money management to psychology to system design.. For extensive free trading information, visit the Web site address listed.

> **TradersCoach.com**
> www.TradersCoach.com
> Contact: Jean McDowell
> 1-800-695-6188
> 1-858-695-0592

Colleagues in Trading: This is a nonprofit organization that provides valuable support and information to traders and investors. Their goal is to be the equivalent to a Good Housekeeping seal of approval for firms in the financial and trading industry. They research and seek out trading products and services that meet their standards of excellence.

In addition, Colleagues in Trading has developed an approach called the Trader's Life Cycle. This enables visitors to the Web site to determine where in the Life Cycle they may currently be, and where they may want to move to. The Web site lists seminars and lectures that are given by trading industry leaders, including Bennett A. McDowell.

Colleagues in Trading
www.colleaguesintrading.com
Contact: Sharon Giriulat

Trader's EXPO and Money Show Trade Shows Plus the Money Show On-line University: The Trader's EXPO trade shows are geared towards the active trader, while the Money Show trade shows are more appropriate for the savvy investor. Both feature an extensive line-up of prominent speakers in the financial industry including Bennett A. McDowell, author of this book.

Attendance to most events is completely free of charge, and the shows generally last two to four days, which give you ample time to participate in a variety of seminars and workshops on a broad range of trading topics, from money management to system design to retirement portfolio tips.

The trade shows are held in cities across the United States (with the exception of the Money Show in London, England). For the latest information on schedule of cities and dates, please refer to the Web site or phone number shown below each listing. We've provided the information that is current at the time of this printing, but as one might expect, this information may become outdated so it is best to go online and confirm current locations and dates.

Another terrific educational source is MoneyShow.com University. You'll find courses that you can take online in the convenience of your own home or office. There are live streaming audio video classes presented by leaders in education, including Bennett A. McDowell. Be sure to take advantage of his course on money management, available to you free of charge.

The Money Show University
www.moneyshow.com

Trader's EXPO—New York City
February of each year
www.tradersexpo.com
800-970-4355

Trader's EXPO—California
Summer of each year
www.tradersexpo.com
800-970-4355

Trader's EXPO—Las Vegas, Nevada
November of each year
www.tradersexpo.com
800-970-4355

The Money Show Tradeshow—Washington, DC
Autumn of each year
www.moneyshow.com/msc/investors/calendar.asp
800-970-4355

The Money Show Tradeshow—San Francisco, California
August of each year
www.moneyshow.com/msc/investors/calendar.asp
800-970-4355

The Money Show Tradeshow—Las Vegas, Nevada
May of each year
www.moneyshow.com/msc/investors/calendar.asp
800-970-4355

The World Money Show Tradeshow—London, England
December of each year
www.moneyshow.com/msc/investors/calendar.asp
800-970-4355

The World Money Show Tradeshow—Orlando, Florida
February of each year
www.moneyshow.com/msc/investors/calendar.asp
800-970-4355

Glossary

accumulation distribution (A/C)   A momentum indicator that attempts to gauge supply and demand by determining whether traders or investors are accumulating (buying) or distributing (selling) a certain financial instrument by identifying divergences between price and volume flow.

American Stock Exchange (AMEX)   The second-largest stock exchange in the United States after the NYSE. Generally, the listing rules are more lenient than those of the NYSE, and therefore the AMEX has a larger representation of stocks and bonds issued by smaller companies. It is located in New York City.

annual percentage rate (APR)   The periodic rate times the number of periods in a year. Example: a 5 percent quarterly return has an APR of 20 percent.

Applied Reality Trading® (ART®)   *Applied Reality Trading* is a technical analysis system developed by Bennett A. McDowell that focuses on trading the realities of the financial markets. The *ART* software works on any time frame and in any market for both investors and day traders. The software generates charts that illustrate clear entry and exit signals and sound money management rules.

APR   See *annual percentage rate*.

***ART* bear price bar**   When prices close on the *lower* half of the bar, it is an *ART* bear price bar. The bar is defined by the relation between the *close* and the price bar interval. The bears are in control at the close of the price bar. (*ART* determines bear and bull differently than other systems.)

***ART* bull price bar**   When prices close on the *upper* half of the bar, it is an *ART* bull price bar. The bar is defined by the relation between the close and the price bar interval. The bulls are in control at the close of the price bar. (*ART* determines bear and bull differently than other systems.)

***ART* elongated price bar**   This price bar is at least one-third longer than the previous three to five price bars.

***ART* inside price bar**   A compressed price bar forming directly after the signal bar in an *ART* reversal. It can be used to aggressively enter an *ART* reversal trade.

ART **neutral price bar**   On this price bar, the open and the close are at the 50 percent point on the bar when it closes. Both bulls and bears are in stalemate at the close of the price bar.

ART **one-bar reversal (1B)**   This scalp signal identifies exact entries and exits. It can also be used for scaling in and scaling out of trends. This reversal signal requires only one price bar that is the signal bar, which determines both the entry and also the stop-loss exit. It can be used on all markets and all time frames.

ART **signal price bar**   Represents the price bar used for a trade entry when using the *ART* reversals. The *ART* trading software designates the *ART* Signal Bar with a 1B or 2B directly above or below the price bar.

ART **two-bar reversal (2B)**   This scalp signal identifies exact entries and exits. It can also be used for scaling in and scaling out of trends. This reversal signal requires two price bars, the first price bar is used for the stop-loss exit and the second price bar or signal bar is used for the entry. It can be used on all markets and all time frames.

ask price   Also known as the offer. The price a seller is willing to accept. The difference between the bid and ask is known as the bid-ask spread.

asset   Any possession that has value in an exchange.

asset allocation   The process of deciding what types of assets you want to own, and the percentage of each. As conditions change, the percent allotted to each asset class changes.

at-the-money   An option is at-the-money if the strike price of the option is equal to the market price of the underlying asset.

average true range (ATR)   Helps determine a market's volatility over a given period. It is calculated by taking an average of the true ranges over a set number of previous periods. It is the (moving) average of the true range for a given period.

backtesting   Backtesting is the use of historical data to test technical or fundamental theories or systems to determine the historical performance of a given set of rules. Backtesting can give information on what the performance would have been but does not guarantee future results. eSignal has a playback feature that enables you to test your trading skills using historical data and playing it forward to determine what your performance would have been. The value of the playback is that you do not see the right side of the chart so you are testing your own ability to make decisions without knowing what the next price bar will bring.

balance sheet   A listing of all assets and liabilities for an individual or a business. The surplus of assets over liabilities is the net worth, or what is owned free of debt.

basis   This is your cost of the asset. If you pay $10 per share for a stock and $1 per share for commission, your basis is $11 per share.

bear   Someone who believes prices will decline and is generally pessimistic about future market returns.

bear market   A market characterized by prolonged broad declining prices. Some negative information has entered the market to create this condition. Generally the downturn in price is in excess of 20 percent. Not to be confused with a correction.

bid–ask spread   The difference between the bid and the ask. The spread narrows or widens according to the supply and demand for the security being traded.

bid price   The price a buyer is willing to pay.

black Monday   Refers to October 19, 1987, when the DJIA fell 508 points after sharp drops the previous week.

black box system   This is a 100 percent mechanical system that requires absolutely NO discretion. The concern with these systems is that they are unable to adapt to ever-changing market cycles. The reality is that over time, all systems require some form of discretionary decision making to be consistently profitable. *ART* is not a black box system.

blue chip company   A large, nationally recognized, financially sound firm with a long track record usually selling high-quality and widely accepted goods and services. Examples: General Electric and IBM.

bond   A debt investment. Investors lend money to an institution by buying bonds and receive fixed interest payments in return. When the bond matures, the investor receives the principal back.

bond market   The bond market, also known as the debt, credit, or fixed income market, is a financial market where participants buy and sell debt securities usually in the form of bonds.

bracketed market   This is also known as a consolidating, range-bound, drunk, choppy, sleepy, channeled, sideways or nontrending market. When a market is bracketed it is stuck in a price range between an identifiable resistance and support level. On a chart, a bracket will be seen as a sideways horizontal line. Some of the most powerful and profitable trends come out of markets that have been bracketed for more than 20 price bars.

breakout   A sharp change in price movement after the market has traded sideways for at least 20 price bars. This is beyond a previous high (or low) or outside the boundaries of a preceding price bracket.

broker   An individual or online firm that is paid a commission for executing customer orders; an agent specializing in stocks, bonds, commodities or options and must be registered with the exchange where the securities are traded.

bull   Someone who believes that prices will rise and is generally optimistic about future market returns.

bull market   A market characterized by prolonged broad rising prices. Positive information has entered the market to create this condition. Over 70 percent of historic periods have been bull markets.

buy   To purchase an asset.

buyers market   A market in which the supply exceeds the demand, creating lower prices.

call   An options contract with the right to buy a specific number of shares of a stock at a specified price (the strike price) on or before a specific expiration date, regardless of the underlying stock's current market price. A call option writer sells the right to a buyer.

candlesticks   A type of bar chart developed by the Japanese, in which the price range between the open and the close is either a white rectangle (if the close is higher) or a black rectangle (if the close is lower).

capital   The money you need to trade or invest. This should be risk capital, meaning that you can afford to lose this money.

cash per share   The amount of cash divided by the total number of common stock shares outstanding for a given stock. A corporation with high cash per share ratio is said to be cash rich and may be considered low risk or undervalued.

central bank   The institution in each country responsible for setting monetary policy, print money, managing reserves, and controlling inflation. In the United States, the central bank is the Federal Reserve System, also known as the Fed.

channeling market   This is also known as a bracketed, consolidating, sideways or non-trending market. See *bracketed market*.

chart   A graph that depicts the price movement of a given market. The most common type of chart is the bar chart, which denotes each interval's open, high, low, and close for a given market with a single price bar.

chart analysis   The study of price charts in an effort to find patterns that in the past preceded price advances or declines. The basic concept is that the development of similar patterns in a current market can signal a probable market move in the same direction. Practitioners of chart analysis are often referred to as *technical analysis* traders or investors.

Chicago Board of Trade (CBOT)   Established in 1848, the CBOT is a leading exchange for futures and options on futures. More than 3,600 CBOT members trade 50 different futures and options products at the exchange through open auction and/or electronically. CME Group is a combined entity formed by the 2007 merger of the Chicago Mercantile Exchange (CME) and the Chicago Board of Trade (CBOT).

Chicago Board Options Exchange (CBOE)   Founded in 1973, the CBOE is an exchange that focuses on options contracts for individual equities, indexes and interest rates. The CBOE is the world's largest options market. It captures a majority of the options traded. It is also a market leader in developing new financial products and technological innovation, particularly with electronic trading.

Chicago Mercantile Exchange (CME)   Founded in 1898 as the Chicago Butter and Egg Board, this is an American financial exchange based in Chicago. Originally the exchange was a not-for-profit organization. The exchange demutualized in November 2000, went public in December 2002, and merged with the Chicago Board of Trade in July 2007. CME trades several types of financial instruments: interest rates, equities, currencies, and commodities. CME has the largest options and futures contracts open interest (number of contracts outstanding) of any future exchange in the world. Trading is conducted in two methods: an open outcry format and the CME Globex® electronic trading platform. Approximately 70 percent of total volume at the exchange occurs on CME Globex.

Chicago Mercantile Group (CME Group)   The world's largest and most diverse exchange. Formed by the 2007 merger of the Chicago Mercantile Exchange (CME) and the Chicago Board of Trade (CBOT), CME Group serves the risk management needs of customers around the globe. As an international marketplace, CME Group brings buyers and sellers together on the CME Globex electronic trading platform and on its trading floors.

choppy market   See *bracketed market.*

churning (excessive trading)   When a broker excessively trades an account for the purpose of increasing his or her commission revenue. This practice is entirely unethical and does not serve the customer's investment or trading goals.

close   The period at the end of the trading session; sometimes refers to the closing price.

commission   Fees paid to a brokerage house to execute a transaction.

commission ratio   Total dollars of commission paid divided by total dollars profit earned equals the commission ratio. This formula is not applicable to traders that are not generating a profit or have a pay off ratio of less than 1 to 1.

commodities   Physical goods that are traded at a futures exchange such as grains, foods, meats, metals, etc.

consolidating market   This is also known as a bracketed, channeled, sideways or nontrending market. See *bracketed market.*

Consumer Price Index (CPI)   Issued by the Bureau of Labor Statistics, this figure is a popularly used measure of inflation. It measures the relative change in prices of a basket of consumer products and services.

contract   A single unit of a commodity or future. This is similar to shares in stocks.

contrarian   One who trades or invests on contrary opinion using the theory that they can profit by doing the opposite of the majority of traders or investors in the market.

correction   A short, sharp reverse in prices during a longer market trend.

corrective Elliott wave   Refers to Elliott wave structure made up of impulsive wave counts and corrective wave counts. Usually refers to a correction wave sequence in an impulsive trend wave sequence.

countertrend trade A trading strategy where an investor or trader attempts to make small gains through a series of trades against the current trend.

cover To liquidate an existing position (such as sell if one is long; buy if one is short).

covered call To sell a call option. At the same time you own the same number of shares represented by the option in the underlying stock.

covered put To sell a put option. At the same time you are holding a short position in the underlying stock.

data Live streaming market data are provided to the trader or investor by data providers and brokerage houses. These data are used to conduct technical analysis and provides price and volume information. Real-time data is sent by the minute during the trading day. Generally data providers charge more for real-time data because they are more labor intensive to provide. Real-time data are used by day traders. End-of-day data are provided at the end of the day and give you final price and volume information for the market you are analyzing. Data providers charge less for end-of-day data, and this type of data is used more by investors and position traders.

day trade A trade that is liquidated on the same day it is initiated.

day trader Day trading refers to the practice of buying and selling financial instruments within the same trading day such that all positions will usually (not necessarily always) be closed before the market close. Traders that participate in day trading are day traders.

debt-to-equity ratio Ratio demonstrating an institution's debt relative to its equity. Just one component used by corporations in assessing optimal capital structures.

decimals Increment of movement in the stock market.

deflation A drop in average product and services price levels, usually caused by excessive tightening of money supply. Deflation can lead to reduced economic demand and higher unemployment. Not to be confused with disinflation.

discretionary trader A trader who makes decisions based on his own analysis of the market, rather than in response to signals generated by a computerized black box system. The best discretionary traders are those who develop a systematic approach and then use discretion in their entries, exits, and position sizing to improve performance.

disinflation The slowing growth of average product and services price levels. This can be thought of as the slowing of inflation. Not to be confused with deflation.

divergence The failure of a market or indicator to follow suit when a related market or indicator sets a new high or low. Some analysts look for divergences as a signal of impending market tops and bottoms.

diversification   Trading or investing in a variety of markets and sectors to reduce risk. Don't put all your eggs in one basket!

dividend   A payment made to stockholders, usually quarterly, out of a firm's current or retained earnings.

DJIA   See *Dow Jones Industrial Average.*

dollar cost averaging   Averaging the cost per share of a particular security by investing a fixed sum regularly.

double witching   A term used for the day when both options and futures expire.

doubling down   Adding on to a losing position.

Dow Jones Industrial Average (DJIA) (Dow)   A price-weighted index of 30 blue-chip U.S. stocks. This index is also known as the Dow.

downtrend   A general tendency for declining prices in a given market.

drawdown   A decrease in the value of your account because of losing trades or because of paper losses, which may occur simply because of a decline in value of open positions. Low drawdown is a desirable performance feature for a trader or investor.

edge   See pay off ratio. This is the advantage you and your system gives you over the market by dollars earned.

e-mini   Used in the futures market to represent a smaller trading market of its parent market.

earnings per share (EPS)   A firm's total after-tax net earnings divided by the number of common shares outstanding.

earnings to price ratio (E/P)   Ratio of a company's earnings per share to its share price. This is the reverse of the price to earnings ratio.

efficient market   The theory that the financial markets quickly and efficiently compensate and price in all widely known information.

Elliott wave analysis   A method of market analysis based on the theories of Ralph Nelson Elliott. Although relatively complex, the basic theory is based on the concept that markets move in waves, forming a general pattern of five waves (or market legs) in the direction of the main trend, followed by three corrective waves in the opposite direction.

entry   The point at which you place or open your trade or investment. This is the opposite of your exit. When placing your entry you should already know what your initial exit will be—see *stop-loss exit.* The distance between your entry and your exit will determine what your trade size will be.

equities markets   Stock markets.

equity   The total dollar value of an account.

equity curve   The value of your account over time, illustrated in a graph.

exchange traded fund (ETF)   A security that tracks a specific index, equity category, or other basket of assets but is traded on an exchange like a single stock.

exercise an option   To buy or sell a call or put option by the expiration date on the options contract.

exit   The point at which you close your trade or investment. This is the opposite of your entry. It can also be known as your *stop-loss exit*. It is a crucial part of your money management risk control plan. The distance between your entry and your exit will determine what your trade size will be.

expiration date   The last day on which an option may be exercised. For stock options, this date is the third Friday of the expiration month.

false breakout   A short-lived price move that penetrates a prior high or low before succumbing to a pronounced price move in the opposite direction. For example, if the price of a stock that has traded between $18 and $20 then rises to $21 and then quickly falls below $18, the move to $21 can be termed a false breakout.

Federal Open Market Committee (FOMC)   A 12-member committee responsible for setting credit and interest rate policy for the Federal Reserve System. They set the discount rate directly and control the federal funds rate by buying and selling government securities impacting the rate. They meet eight times a year under the direction of a chairman.

Federal Reserve board of governors   The governing arm of the Federal Reserve System, which seeks to regulate the economy through the implementation of monetary policy. The seven members of the board of governors are appointed by U.S. presidents to serve 14-year terms.

Federal Reserve System (Fed)   The United States central banking system, responsible for regulating the flow of money and credit. It serves as a bank for other banks and the U.S. government.

Fibonacci retracements   The concept that retracements of prior trends will often approximate 38.2 percent and 61.8 percent—numbers derived from the Fibonacci sequence.

Fibonacci sequence   A sequence of numbers that begins with 1,1 and progresses to infinity, with each number in the sequence equal to the sum of the preceding two numbers. Thus, the initial numbers in the sequence would be 1, 1, 2, 3, 5, 8, 13, 21, 34, 55, 89, etc. The ratio of consecutive numbers in the sequence converges to 0.618 as the numbers get larger. The ratio of alternate numbers in the sequence (for example, 21 and 55) converges to 0.382 as the numbers get larger. These two ratios—0.618 and 0.382—are commonly used to project retracements of prior price swings.

fill   The price at which an order is executed is considered a fill. For example, if a trade was placed at $32.00 and filled at $32.25 the fill price would be $32.25.

filter   An indicator that selects only data that meet specific criteria. Too many filters can lead to overoptimization.

financial instruments   This is a term used to denote any form of funding medium. They can be categorized by whether they are cash instruments or derivative instruments. Cash instruments are financial instruments whose value is determined directly by markets. They can be divided into securities, which are readily transferable, and other cash instruments such as loans and deposits, where both borrower and lender have to agree on a transfer. Derivative instruments are financial instruments that derive their value from some other financial instrument or variable. They can be divided into exchange-traded derivatives and over-the-counter (OTC) derivatives. If it is debt, it can be further categorized into short term (less than one year) or long term. Foreign exchange instruments and transactions are neither debt nor equity based and belong in their own category.

flat   When you are not in the market with a live position or when you close out all your positions before end of the trading day you are considered flat.

floor trader   A member of the exchange who trades on the floor for personal profit.

forecasts   Individuals that attempt to predict future market behavior are said to be forecasting the market. They tend to use indicators such as MACD, stochastic and Elliott waves to determine their forecasts. Forecasting the markets is often like forecasting the weather; it is difficult to do with any consistent accuracy.

FOREX market   The foreign exchange market exists wherever one currency is traded for another. It is by far the largest financial market in the world, and includes trading between large banks, central banks, currency speculators, multinational corporations, governments, and other financial markets and institutions.

fundamental analysis   The use of economic data and news data to analyze financial markets. For example, fundamental analysis of a currency might focus on such items as relative inflation rates, interest rates, economic growth rates, and political factors. In evaluating a stock, a fundamental analyst would look at financials, value, earnings, debt, management, operations, competition and other relative data. Fundamental analysis is often contrasted with technical analysis, and some investors and traders use a combination of the two.

futures   When commodity exchanges added stock index contracts and currency contracts, the term futures was developed to be more inclusive.

futures market   An auction market in which participants buy and sell commodity/future contracts for delivery on a specified future date. Trading is carried on through open yelling and hand signals in a trading pit.

Gann analysis   Market analysis based on a variety of technical concepts developed by William Gann, a famous stock and commodity trader during the first half of the twentieth century.

gap   A price zone at which no trades occur. For example, if a market that has previously traded at a high of $20 per share opens at $22 on the following day. The price zone between $20 and $22 is referred to as a gap-up. If the price zone were to go from $22 to $20 it would be a gap-down. Sometimes Fed announcements or corporate earnings announcements can create an immediate gap even in the middle of a trading day.

Globex®   Today the CME Globex trading system operates at the heart of CME. Proposed in 1987, it was introduced in 1992 as the first global electronic trading platform for futures contracts. This fully electronic trading system allows market participants to trade from booths at the exchange or while sitting in a home or an office thousands of miles away.

good 'til canceled (GTC)   By choosing GTC, your order will remain open until it is executed or canceled, regardless of the number of trading days.

gross domestic product (GDP)   The monetary value of all products and services produced in a country over a certain time period. In the United States, the GDP's growth is a popularly used indicator of overall economic health.

grounded assessments   These are trading and investing rules that are based on reality versus forecasts or predictions. For example, trade and investment entries based on price and volume would be considered grounded assessments. The ART signals are all grounded assessments.

hedge   To reduce risk in an investment or trade by offsetting it with another investment or trade.

hedge fund   A managed portfolio of investments that is generally unregulated (unlike a mutual fund) and may invest in any highly speculative markets, including options.

hedger   A market participant who implements a position to reduce price risk. The hedger's risk position is exactly opposite that of the speculator, who accepts risk in implementing positions to profit from anticipated price moves.

high probability   Trades or investments that statistically have a higher probability for success.

higher time-frame filter   A filter technique used to look at the market you are trading or investing in on a higher time frame to see if it confirms your primary time frame.

hyperbolic move   A sharp and significant move to the up or down side of your position. You might decide to *scale out* of a position to lock in profit if this type of move occurs.

immediate or cancel (IOC)   By choosing IOC, your order will have immediate execution of all or part of the quantity of stock you specified. Any portion of the order that is not executed immediately is automatically canceled.

impulsive Elliott wave   The major trend in every time frame takes the form of five waves (impulse waves) that, once complete, are corrected by three waves (corrective waves).

index fund   A mutual fund that tracks a stated market index.

individual retirement account (IRA)   A retirement account any employed person (or spouse of an employed person) can open and contribute to. Assets in the account grow tax deferred and contributions may be tax deductible. Distributions taken before age 59 are subject to penalty.

inflation   Rate of increase in average product and service price levels. Different indexes use different baskets of products and services to compute the average prices. A popular index is the Consumer Price Index.

initial public offering (IPO)   The first sale of equities (stocks) to the public by a private firm. In making an IPO, a private firm has gone public.

insider trading   Trading by officers, directors, major stockholders or others who hold private inside information allowing them to benefit from buying or selling stock. It is a misuse of inside information to profit more quickly than the average shareholder would.

institutional investor   A bank, mutual fund, pension fund, or other corporate entity that trades financial instruments in large volumes.

intra-day time frame   A shorter time frame from the 1-minute to the 60-minute that day traders use in making their entry and exit decisions.

investing   This is a term with several closely related meanings in business management, finance, and economics, related to saving or deferring consumption. An asset is usually purchased, or equivalently a deposit is made in a bank, in hopes of getting a future return or interest from it. Literally, the word means the action of putting something into somewhere else. Think of it as using financial instruments to invest savings for future gain; it usually is not considered a short-term endeavor.

investor   Generally uses a buy-and-hold approach using weekly and monthly charts to evaluate the market. An investor can be a trader when timing long-term investments. Investors are more likely to incorporate fundamental analysis into their approach than a day-trader would.

in-the-money   When an option's current market price is above the strike price of a call, or below the strike price of a put. An in-the-money option would produce a profit, if exercised.

Kelly formula   See *optimal f formula.*

large cap   Refers to the size of a firm's market capitalization. Generally, any firms with a market cap above $10 billion are referred to as a large cap.

left brain   The human brain is divided into two hemispheres, the left and the right, each of which is responsible for specific functions in human behavior and existence. The left brain is responsible primarily for speech, logic, planning, and analysis abilities. It tends to think in words as opposed to pictures and looks at the details as opposed to the big picture. Those of us who are analytical and scientific in nature are generally referred to as left-brain thinkers.

leverage The ability to control a dollar amount of a commodity or financial instrument greater than the amount of personal capital employed. This ability is obtained by using borrowed money, such as a margin account. The greater the leverage of the position, the greater the potential is for profit or loss.

limit order This is an order in which you can set the maximum price you want to pay for your purchase, or a minimum price you will accept as a seller.

limit position For many futures contracts, government regulations specify a maximum position size (such as number of contracts) that a speculator may hold.

limit price move For many futures contracts, the exchanges specify a maximum amount by which the price can change on a single day. A market that increases in price by this specified maximum is said to be limit-up, while a market that declines by the maximum is said to be limit-down.

liquid market A market in which there are a large number of trades daily so that most buy and sell orders can be executed without dramatically moving prices. In other words, a liquid market allows you the ease of entry and exit.

liquidity The degree to which a given market is liquid. When volume is high, there is usually a lot of liquidity. Low liquidity in markets can result in poor fills.

liquidity risk Risk when you enter a trade, which you may not have sufficient liquidity to exit at your desired exit point.

long A position established with a buy order, which profits in a rising price market. The term is also used to refer to the person or entity holding such a position.

long call To buy a call option.

long put To buy a put option.

lot The quantity of shares in which stocks are bought or sold. In futures markets, a lot is called a *contract*.

MACD See *moving average convergence/divergence.*

margin To borrow money from a financial provider (broker or bank) to purchase certain financial instruments.

margin call A Federal Reserve board and financial service provider requirement that you deposit additional funds or sell some of your holdings to increase the equity in your margin account if it has fallen below the minimum.

margin debit The amount of money borrowed from a financial service provider.

margin risk Risk where you can lose more than the dollar amount in your margined trading account.

market index This is the weighted average of companies comprising an index. The index represents a category or market (such as the S&P 500 or the NASDAQ).

market maker A broker, bank, or firm such as Goldman Sachs or Merrill Lynch, which buys or sells a security, currency, or futures contract.

market order Order to execute a purchase or sale for the best price available at the time the order is received.

market risk Uncontrolled risk possibilities that are always present in open trade and investment positions are considered market risk. Economic and world events can cause market risk where the market could move so quickly that you may not be able to exit at your stop-loss exit point.

Minneapolis Grain Exchange (MGEX) This exchange was founded as a not-for-profit membership organization and maintains that structure today with a membership base of 390 outstanding seats, or memberships. In 1883, MGEX launched its first futures contract, hard red spring wheat, which is the exchange's most heavily traded product today.

minor pyramid trading point® **(MP)** An MP indicates a correction in the dominant trend.

momentum investing and trading Momentum represents the change in price now from some fixed time period in the past. This strategy attempts to capture short-term price movements based on the belief that price patterns are indicative of future results.

money flow index (MFI) A volume-weighted momentum indicator that measures the strength of money flowing in and out of a financial instrument. It compares *positive* money flow to *negative* money flow to create an indicator that can be compared to price in order to identify the strength or weakness of a trend. The MFI is measured on a 0 to 100 scale and is often calculated using a 14-day period.

money management The use of various methods of risk control in trading and investing. These methods include: (1) using proper trade size; (2) not risking more than 2 percent of your risk account on any one trade; and (3) diversifying your trading or investing account over a number of markets and sectors. This is also known as *risk management.*

moving average (MA) An average of data for a certain number of time periods. It moves because for each calculation, we use the latest number of time periods' data. By definition, a moving average lags the market. An exponentially smoothed moving average (EMA) gives greater weight to the more recent data, in an attempt to reduce the lag time.

moving average convergence/divergence (MACD) This is an indicator developed by Gerald Appel. It is calculated by subtracting the 26-period exponential moving average of a given financial instrument from its 12-period exponential moving average. By comparing moving averages, MACD displays trend following characteristics, and by plotting the difference of the moving averages as an oscillator, MACD displays momentum characteristics. The MACD histogram is the visual representation of the difference between the MACD line and the MACD signal line.

mutual fund   An investment company investing in a variety of securities as dictated by the specific fund's prospectus. Investors do not own the underlying investments; they buy shares of the fund itself.

naked option   A short option position by a trader who does not own the underlying commodity or financial instrument.

naked put   A put option in which the seller does not own the short position. Loss potential is total except for the premium.

narrowing the spread   Reducing the difference between the bid and ask prices of a security.

NASDAQ   See *National Association of Securities Dealers Automated Quotations System.*

NASDAQ 100 index   A modified capitalization-weighted index designed to track the performance of the 100 largest and most actively traded nonfinancial domestic and international securities listed on the NASDAQ.

National Association of Securities Dealers Automated Quotations System (NASDAQ)   The NASDAQ is an American stock market. It was founded in 1971 by the NASD, who divested themselves of it in a series of sales in 2000 and 2001. It is owned and operated by the NASDAQ Stock Market, Inc. the stock of which was listed on its own stock exchange in 2002. NASDAQ is the largest electronic screen-based equity securities market in the United States. With approximately 3,200 companies, it lists more companies and on average trades more shares per day than any other United States market.

National Association of Securities Dealers, Inc. (NASD)   This self-regulatory organization of the securities industry is responsible for the regulation of the NASDAQ stock market and the over-the-counter markets.

nearest month   The expiration date of an option or future that is closest to the present.

net asset value (NAV)   This is an increment of movement in the mutual fund market.

net worth   Total assets minus total liabilities equals net worth.

New York Cotton Exchange (NYCE)   Was founded in 1870 by a group of 100 cotton brokers and merchants in New York City. The oldest commodities exchange in the city, well into the twentieth century, cotton was a leading American commodity for both export and domestic consumption.

New York Futures Exchange (NYFE)   An exchange on which trading occurs for Treasury bond futures and some currency futures.

New York Mercantile Exchange (NYMEX)   This is the world's largest physical commodity futures exchange, located in New York City. Its two principal divisions are the NYMEX and the New York Commodities Exchange (COMEX), which were once independent companies but are now merged.

New York Stock Exchange (NYSE)   Known as the *Big Board*, this is a New York City based stock exchange. The NYSE provides an efficient method for buyers and sellers to trade shares of stock in companies registered for public trading. The exchange provides efficient price discovery via an auction environment designed to produce the fairest price for both parties. As of January 24, 2007 all NYSE stocks can be traded via its electronic hybrid market (except for a small group of very high priced stocks). Customers can now send orders for immediate electronic execution or route orders to the floor for trade in the auction market. In excess of 50 percent of all order flow is now delivered to the floor electronically.

nontrending market   This is also known as a bracketed, consolidating, channeled or sideways market. See *bracketed market*.

NYSE Composite Index   A capitalization-weighted index designed to track the performance of all common stocks listed on the New York Stock Exchange.

OBV   See *on balance volume*.

on balance volume (OBV)   This method is used in technical analysis to detect momentum, the calculation of which relates volume to price change. OBV provides a running total of volume and shows whether this volume is flowing in or out of a given financial instrument. It attempts to detect when a stock, bond, etc. is being accumulated by a large number of buyers or sold by many sellers. Joe Granville developed this indicator.

open interest   In futures markets, the total number of open and short positions are always equal. This total (long or short) is called the open interest. By definition, when a contract month first begins trading, the open interest is zero. The open interest then builds to a peak and declines as positions are liquidated, approaching its expiration date.

open order   An order to buy or sell a security that remains in effect until it is either canceled by the customer or executed.

opening (OPG)   At the opening, by choosing OPG, your order will be executed at the opening price. If it is not executed at the opening, it will be canceled automatically.

Optimal *f* formula   This formula calculates for you the optimum fraction of capital, or percent of capital, to risk on any one trade based on your win ratio and pay off ratio. It gives you a more aggressive calculation than the risk-of-ruin tables do. It is sometimes referred to as the Kelly formula.

optimization   This refers to optimizing software and the process of discovering what impact is the result of varying a particular parameter across different values, then using that information to make an informed decision about which specific parameter values to use in actual trading or investing.

options   The right to buy or sell an underlying asset at a fixed price up to some specified date in the future. The right to buy is a *call option*, and the right to sell is a *put option*.

options market   This is an open market to trade options.

oscillator   Most oscillators go from 0 to 100. Analysts believe that when the indicator is near zero, the price is oversold, and that when the price is near 100 it is overbought.

overtrading   You are overtrading when your commission fees are eating into your profit or when you feel out of control. Stop and reverse (SAR) traders can overtrade because of the speed of their entries and exits.

overbought/oversold indicator   An indicator that attempts to define when prices have risen (or fallen) too far, too fast, and hence are vulnerable to a reaction in the opposite direction.

out-of-the-money   When an option's current market price is below the strike price of a call or above the strike price of a put.

Pacific Stock Exchange (PCX)   This was a regional stock exchange located in San Francisco, California. Its history begins with the founding of the San Francisco Stock and Bond exchange in 1882. Seven years later, the Los Angeles Oil Exchange was founded. In 1957, the two exchanges merged to form the Pacific Coast Stock exchange, though trading floors were kept in both original cities. A name change to the Pacific Stock Exchange took place in 1973. Options trading began three years later. In 1997, *Stock* was dropped from the exchange's name. In 1999, the Pacific Exchange was the first U.S. stock exchange to demutualize. In 2001, the Los Angeles trading floor was closed, and the next year the San Francisco trading floor was closed as well. Pacific Exchange equities trading now takes place exclusively through NYSE Arca (formerly known as ArcaEx), an Electronic Communications Network. In 2003, the Pacific Exchange launched PCX plus, an electronic options trading platform.

paper gain   Unrealized capital gain on securities held based on a comparison of the current market price to the original cost.

paper loss   Unrealized capital loss on securities held based on a comparison of the current market price to the original cost.

pattern recognition   A price-forecasting method that uses historical chart patterns to draw analogies to current situations.

pay off ratio   Average winning trade divided by average losing trade equals the pay off ratio. For example a 2 to 1 pay off ratio means that you are winning two dollars for every one dollar you lose.

P/E ratio   See *price-to-earnings ratio.*

percentage in point (PIP)   The increment of movement in the FOREX market.

pit   The area where a futures contract is traded on the exchange floor.

playback feature   See *backtesting.*

position   Your financial stake in a given financial instrument or market.

position trader   Uses daily and weekly charts on which to base decisions and holds positions for days, weeks, or months.

price   In trading and investing, *price* refers to the last trade price.

price bar   The price bar represents the high and low price behavior in a measured time interval. Price bars can represent different time frames (intervals) such as one-minute, five-minute, daily, weekly, and so on.

price oscillator (PPO) histogram   This is an indicator based on the difference between two moving averages, and is expressed as either a percentage or in absolute terms. The plot is presented as a histogram so that centerline crossovers and divergences are easily identifiable. The same principles apply to the MACD histogram.

price gap   See *gap.*

price-to-earnings (P/E) ratio   The current price of a stock divided by the company's annual earnings. One of the most commonly used stock valuation ratios.

profit margin   An indictor of profitability. Determined by dividing net income by revenue for the same 12-month period. Also known as *net profit margin.*

put-call ratio   The ratio of the volume of put options traded to the volume of call options traded, which is used as an indicator of investor sentiment (bullish or bearish).

psychology   Mastering the psychology of trading and investing is a crucial part of becoming successful. The Trader's Mindset is our definition of what you will attain when you have mastered your financial psychology. Some of the challenges in developing strong psychology are overcoming fear, greed, ego, and anger when trading and investing.

PTP apex   The apex always points in the direction of the trend and is the point of the pyramid (triangle). It will tell you where to enter based on current market dynamics.

PTP base leg   The base leg is the flat base of the pyramid (triangle) and tells you where you will set your stop-loss exit based on current market dynamics.

PTP confirmed   When the market moves beyond the PTP apex in the direction of the trend, it will be confirmed. At that moment, the triangle will turn either *green* or *red*, depending if it is a bull or bear trend.

PTP minscore   This adjustable setting on the *ART* software determines the number of pyramids you will see on your chart.

PTP potential   When the pyramid is potential, it will be *yellow* in color. Once the market moves beyond the apex of the pyramid it will then be confirmed and will turn either *green* or *red*, depending on whether it is a bull or bear trend. If the market does not confirm the pyramid by exceeding the apex, the yellow pyramid (triangle) will disappear.

PTP voided   If a potential *yellow* pyramid is not confirmed, it will be voided and will disappear.

put   An options contract with the right to sell a security at a specified exercise price on or before a specific expiration date.

put option   This is the right to sell a stock (or bond or commodity) at a certain price by a certain date. A put option writer sells the right to a buyer. If the option exercises, the buyer puts the stock to the writer, and the writer must buy it.

primary pyramid trading point® (P)   This *ART* signal indicates entries and exits into a primary trend trade or investment.

pyramid trading point® (PTP)   This *ART* trend trading signal was developed by Bennett A. McDowell and identifies exact entries and exits. It enables you to trade and invest utilizing the *realities* of the markets. It can be used on all markets and all time frames.

rally (Recovery)   An upward movement of prices.

range-bound market   See *bracketed market.*

reality-based trading   Living in reality is to be seeing and reacting to the environment as they are occurring, without attempting to predict future events. When traders are living in reality, they are dealing with what is actually occurring to them at any given moment. When trading and investing in reality, they are focusing on the current moment. They are devoid of opinions and other past or future distractions or thoughts. Reality-based trading and investing involves looking at what is real in the market, such as *price* and *volume.*

recession   A contraction in the business cycle, usually manifesting in slow or negative GDP growth.

relative strength indicator (RSI)   An indicator developed by J. Wells Wilder Jr. that is used to ascertain overbought and oversold conditions. It works on a scale of 99 to 1, with 99 being the strongest and 1 being the weakest. In the stock market, a measure of a given stock's price strength—relative to a broad index of stocks. The term can also be used in a more general sense to refer to an overbought/oversold type of indicator.

resistance level   In technical analysis, a price area at which a rising market is expected to encounter increased selling pressure sufficient to stall or reverse the advance.

retracement   A price movement in the opposite direction of the previous trend. A retracement is usually a price correction. For example, in a rising market, a

55 percent retracement would indicate a price decline equal to 55 percent of the prior advance.

return on investment (ROI)   Book income as a proportion of net book value.

reward-to-risk ratio   The average winning trade divided by the size of the average losing trade. This formula will enable you to determine the estimated potential loss or gain of future transactions. Provided that you have more winners than losers, a ratio of three is excellent.

right brain   The human brain is divided into two hemispheres, the left and right, each of which is responsible for specific functions in human behavior and existence. The right brain is considered to be primarily responsible for feelings, emotions, and creativity. The right brain tends to think in pictures as opposed to words and is able to look at the big picture as opposed to minute detail. Those of us that are more creative tend to be considered right-brain thinkers.

right side of the chart   When trading the live market, the right side of the chart is the unknown. Hindsight is 20/20, and when in the live market there is always uncertainty as to where the market actually will go.

risk   The chance of being wrong about an investment or trade.

risk control   See money management.

ROI   See *return on investment.*

RSI   See *relative strength indicator.*

Russell 2000 index   A capitalization-weighted index designed to track the performance of the 2000 smallest U.S. stocks included in the Russell 3000 Index.

Russell 3000 index   A capitalization-weighted index designed to track the performance of the 3000 larges and most liquid U.S. stocks.

S&P   See *Standard & Poors.*

S&P 500 Composite Stock Price Index   A capitalization-weighted index designed to track the performance of the 500 stocks of the S&P 500. Stocks are included in the index based on their liquidity, market cap, and sector. While not necessarily the 500 largest U.S. companies, these are generally the 500 most widely held.

S&P e-mini   Often abbreviated to e-mini and designated by the commodity ticker symbol ES, a stock market index futures contract traded on the Chicago Mercantile Exchange's Globex electronic trading platform.

SAR   See *stop and reverse.*

scaling in   Refers to adding onto your current trade position to increase your *trade size.* Only *scale in* if the trade or investment is already profitable.

scaling out   Exiting 30 percent of your position when your trading rules tell you to. This is a technique that is effective in reducing stress and locking in profit.

scalper   A trader who seeks to profit from very small price fluctuations. They buy and sell quickly to make a quick profit. They often use *stop and reverse* (SAR) techniques. They can trade larger trade sizes than trend traders and still maintain proper risk control.

seasonal trading   Trading based on consistent, predictable changes in price during the year due to production cycles or demand cycles.

SEC   See *Securities and Exchange Commission.*

sector   Used to characterize a group of securities that are similar with respect to maturity, type, rating, and/or industry.

securities   Also known as *stocks.*

Securities and Exchange Commission (SEC)   The federal agency that is designed to promote full public disclosure and protect the investing public against fraudulent practices in the securities markets.

seller's market   A market in which demand exceeds supply. As a result, the seller can dictate the price and terms of a sale.

sell off   The sale of securities under pressure.

set-up   When your trading rules identify certain criteria that must be present prior to entering the market.

share   This is a unit of measure for financial instruments including stocks, mutual funds, limited partnerships, and REITs.

shareholder   A person or entity that owns shares or equity in a corporation.

short   When you sell before you have bought the item, you are *shorting* the market. This position is implemented with a sale, which profits from a declining price market. The term also refers to the trader or entity holding such a position.

short call   When you sell a call option that you don't already own.

short put   To sell a *put option.*

sideways market   Also known as a bracketed, consolidating, channeled, or non-trending market. See *bracketed market.*

slippage   The difference in price between what you expect to pay when you enter the market and what you actually pay. For example, if you attempt to buy at 20 and you end up buying at 20.5, you have a half point of slippage.

small cap   Refers to the relative size of a firm's market capitalization. Traditionally, any firm with a market cap under $10 billion is referred to as small cap.

speculator   A person who willingly accepts risk by buying and selling financial instruments or commodities in the hopes of profiting from anticipated price movements.

split   The division of outstanding shares of a corporation into a larger or smaller number of shares. For example: In a three-for-one split, each holder of 100 shares before would now have 300 shares.

spread   The difference between the bid price and the ask price.

Standard & Poor's Corporation (S&P)   A company well known for its rating of stocks and bonds according to investment risk (the Standard & Poor's rating) and for compiling the Standard & Poor's Index.

stochastic   An overbought-oversold indicator, made popular by George Lane, which is based on the observation that prices close near the high of the day in an uptrend. In a downtrend, they close near the low of the day.

stock   A financial instrument that signifies an ownership position in a corporation. Stock is the capital raised by a corporation through the issuance of shares. A person that holds at least a partial share of stock is called a *shareholder*.

stock market   This is a market for the trading and investing in company stock that is a security listed on a stock exchange.

stop and reverse (SAR)   Used to close the current trade and open a new trade in the opposite direction.

stop limit order   An order that is triggered when the stop price is reached but can only be executed at the limit price.

stop-loss exit   Also referred to as a stop, initial stop, or trailing stop. It is your designated price level where you have determined you must exit your trade if it goes against you. It is used to help control your *trade risk*. This is the worst case scenario if the trade or investment does go against you. It is important to determine the exit point *before* entering the trade or investment.

stop order   A buy order placed above the market (or sell order placed below the market) that becomes a market order when the specified price is reached.

stopped out   A purchase or sale executed under a stop order at the stop price specified by the customer.

straddle   The purchase or sale of an equal number of puts and calls with the same terms at the same time.

strike price   This is the fixed price of an option.

supply = demand   When supply equals demand, both the seller and buyer agree on price but disagree on value.

support level   In technical analysis, a price area at which a falling market is expected to encounter increased buying support sufficient to stall or reverse the decline.

swing trading   Short-term trading approach designed to capture quick moves in the market.

technical analysis   Price forecasting methods based on a study of price itself (and volume) as opposed to the underlying fundamental (such as economic) market factors. Technical analysis traders and investors use charts to detect patterns in the market. Technical analysis is often contrasted with fundamental analysis, and some investors and traders use a combination of the two.

The Trader's Assistant™   A complete trade posting and trade record keeping system created by Bennett A. McDowell to streamline your trading and keep you organized by recording all trade information on trade posting cards and trade ledgers.

the trader's mindset   See *psychology*.

tick   The increment of movement and price fluctuation up or down in the futures market is called a tick.

ticker symbol   Standard abbreviation used to refer to a stock when placing orders or conducting research.

time frame   The time frame is represented by a price bar interval time such as two-minute chart, daily chart, and so on.

trade   When a buyer and seller agree on price but disagree on value a trade occurs. More simply stated, it is the point where the value of selling and the value of receiving are equal and the trade occurs.

trade risk   The risk traders attempt to control through money management and risk control.

trade size   This is also known as *position size*. It is the size of your trade or investment represented in the number of units (shares, contracts, etc.) of the market you are trading or investing in. Selecting optimal trade size is important in maintaining solid risk control.

Trade Size Calculator™   Risk control software created by Bennett A. McDowell to determine a trader's maximum *trade size* based on certain variables such as percent risk and equity account size.

trading   Opening a position in a financial market, either long or short, with the plan of closing it out at a substantial profit. If the trade goes against you, the plan is to cut losses quickly by using effective risk control.

trailing stop   This stop-loss exit moves in the direction of a trend trade, locking in profit in either a long or short trend.

transaction   The delivery of a security by a seller and its acceptance by the buyer.

trend   The tendency of prices to move in a given general direction (up or down).

trend channel   A trend line or series of trend lines used to identify upward or downward sloping trends by placing the trend lines on the highs and lows of the channel.

trend exhaustion   When a trend ends it has reached trend exhaustion. With the *ART* system, trend exhaustion generally occurs after four to five consecutive *primary pyramid trading points* in the same direction.

trend trader   The trend trader trades or invests in the direction of the overall trend.

trending day   A day that continued primarily in one trend direction, either up or down, from open to close.

true range   The greatest of the difference between the current high and the current low, or the difference between the current high and the previous close, or the difference between the current low and the previous close.

ungrounded assessments   Trading and investing rules that try to forecast or predict the market. For example, MACD, stochastic and Elliott wave are ungrounded assessments.

unrealized gain   The appreciation in value of an asset that has not been sold—paper gains.

unrealized loss   The depreciation in value of an asset that has not been sold—paper loss.

uptrend   A general tendency for rising prices in a given market.

volatility   Refers to the range of prices in a given time period. A highly volatile market has a large range in daily prices, whereas a low-volatility market has a small range of daily prices. This is a measure of price variability in a market. A volatile market is a market that is subject to wide price fluctuations.

volume   The total number of shares or contracts traded during a given period.

whipsaw   A price pattern characterized by repeated, abrupt reversals in trend. The term is often used to describe losses resulting from a choppy or trendless market.

win ratio   Number of winning trades divided by the total number of trades equals the win ratio. Example a win ratio of 60 percent means you have 60 percent winning trades.

About The Author

Bennett A. McDowell, founder of TradersCoach.com®, began his financial career on Wall Street in 1984, and later became a "Registered Securities Broker" and "Financial Advisor" for Prudential Securities and Morgan Stanley.

As a financial advisor, Bennett's niche was "Active Trading" and "Investing" for a community of high net worth clients using his own proprietary trading system. This system later became known as the *Applied Reality Trading*®, or the *ART*®, system.

Bennett brought the *ART* software to the public in the year 2003. This was in answer to his clients' many requests for him to share with them his successful trading and investing techniques. Today the *ART* system is used in over 40 countries around the world by sophisticated hedge fund managers, individual investors and active traders alike.

Considered an expert in technical analysis and complex trading platforms, Bennett lectures nationally and writes articles for many leading trading publications including *Technical Analysis of Stocks & Commodities* magazine. Internationally recognized as a leader in trading education, Bennett teaches trading to students worldwide through his company *TradersCoach.com*.

He is honored to be included as a member of the *eSignal* "Trading With The Masters" team. In addition, *TradersCoach.com, Applied Reality Trading*, and *The Traders Assistant*® Record Keeping System have received numerous *Stocks & Commodities* magazine Readers' Choice Awards.

Bennett resides in San Diego, CA with his wife and two children. He can be reached by e-mail via Team@TradersCoach.com.

Index

Printed in the USA/Agawam, MA
April 6, 2022

791391.009